DAVID &
CHARLES
BRITAIN

Snowdonia

Snowdonia

William Condry

David & Charles
Newton Abbot   London   North Pomfret (Vt)

Title page The great cliffs of Clogwyn y Garnedd, the east face of Snowdon, are a mixture of slaty and volcanic rocks which yield enough calcium to support a varied community of lime-loving plants

More titles in this series:
The Yorkshire Dales
Geoffrey N. Wright

**The Pembrokeshire Coast
National Park**
Dillwyn Miles

Forthcoming titles:
The Lake District
Michael Dunn

The Northumbrian Uplands
Geoffrey N. Wright

British Library Cataloguing in Publication Data

Condry, William
  Snowdonia.
  1. Snowdonia National Park (Wales)——
  Description and travel——Guide-books
  I. Title
  914.29′2504858   DA740.S6

  ISBN 0-7153-8734-0

Text & illustrations © William Condry 1987

Phototypeset by ABM Typographics Limited, Hull
and printed in Great Britain
by Butler & Tanner Ltd, Frome
for David & Charles Publishers plc
Brunel House   Newton Abbot   Devon

Published in the United States of America
by David & Charles Inc
North Pomfret   Vermont 05053   USA

CONTENTS

AUTHOR'S PREFACE

My memories of Snowdonia go back to early childhood. In July 1923, my mother, who was a great enthusiast for the out-of-doors, brought my sister, myself and several friends to camp in the lee of the sand-dunes at Talybont, north of Barmouth. No caravans had as yet appeared on that coast and even tents were uncommon. We came by train from Birmingham. It rained all the way and even the smallest hills had retreated into the clouds. Our camping gear went by horse and cart from Talybont station to the waterlogged site. Somehow, despite the wind and the rain, we erected the very awkward, tall, square tent, ate an improvised meal and went to bed with little hope that our new home would stand up to the storm.

But during the night the depression moved away, the morning was windstill and clear and we were thrilled to discover that all along the inland view there stretched a range of exciting mountains – the first we children had ever seen. For my five-year-old mind it was a simple case of love at first sight and although I have seen many fine mountains since then, my early feelings of enchantment over Snowdonia have never faded.

When I grew up I lost no time in coming to live in Wales, always in or close to Snowdonia, and no matter what preoccupations have filled the years, this beautiful region has remained a marvellous background to my life. When time has allowed I have climbed all the summits from Foel Fras in the north to Tarren Hendre in the south; I have plodded joyously across the wide moorlands, admired the lakes, rivers and waterfalls and found happiness in the wooded valleys, on the sea cliffs and in the wide dunelands.

From my earliest years I have been fascinated by wildlife and wild places and these days I still get no keener delight than to clamber up the mountain slopes to reach the higher cliffs and see those entrancing and sometimes rare flowers and ferns which belong exclusively to the alpine zone. I have seen such plants in far greater magnificence in the mountains of Switzerland but they did not give me greater joy than those I find today in the crags and gullies of Snowdonia.

From the natural history of plants and animals to that of man is a very short step. In my wanderings in Snowdonia I have always been conscious of the region's earlier inhabitants and of the many traces of their living and their dying. All down prehistory and history the succeeding generations have left behind them enough clues to quicken our interest and make us want to find out more about their lifestyles, their failures, their successes, no matter who or what they were – hunters, fishers, food-gatherers, farmers, miners, soldiers or anything else. In this book I have tried to point out what has most interested me about both the wildlife-story and the human life-story of Snowdonia. I hope that what I have said will help others to enjoy Snowdonia as much as I have. But let us not take this marvellous Park for granted. Its would-be exploiters and desecrators are never far away and against them it needs to be eternally defended. We can each help the Park in our own preferred way either by supporting one or more of the conservation bodies or perhaps by other means at our disposal. What is vital is that we should all do something to rally public opinion behind the National Parks ideal.

Many friends have been generous with information for this book and I am very happy to thank them all. I am indebted also to the staffs of the National Park Authority, the Nature Conservancy Council, the British Geological Survey, the Gwynedd county archivists and the National Trust for help and advice. The National Library of Wales has, as always, proved an unfailing source of books; so, too, has the Dyfed County Library.

INTRODUCTION

There is a well-trodden path from Ogwen at the head of the Nant Ffrancon Pass up into the wild corrie of Cwm Idwal. It leads you along the banks of a tarn in whose flawless mirror great cliffs and towering buttresses are reflected. Then on you go under huge slabby rocks with hard smooth faces which slant upwards to unseen heights. Like an ant in a basin of sugar lumps you find yourself clambering amongst a chaos of mountainside ruin, up and up to where the crags, which at first seemed impregnable, have split apart just enough for you to scramble up through them and reach the moorland rim. You skirt another small lake, one of the highest in Wales, and soon find yourself in another battle with hillside stones, but smaller this time and more negotiable. Nor is it now a scree under high, impending crags but one that goes far up an open slope with only blue sky and sailing white clouds above. For half an hour you toil upward with stony slides under your feet. But your reward is that ever greater scenery is building up all round, fresh distances unfolding. If you straighten up and look back you see that new mountains have appeared and that there is a gleam of sun on ocean far in the north-west beyond all Anglesey. At last the steepness eases and across a wide stretch of pebbly bareness you come up to the bony, barren top of Glyder Fawr.

You have reached the highest point of your walk, a place which, perhaps as nowhere else, will show you the beauty and magnificence of these uplands. For this Glyder is central amongst Snowdonia's loftiest

9

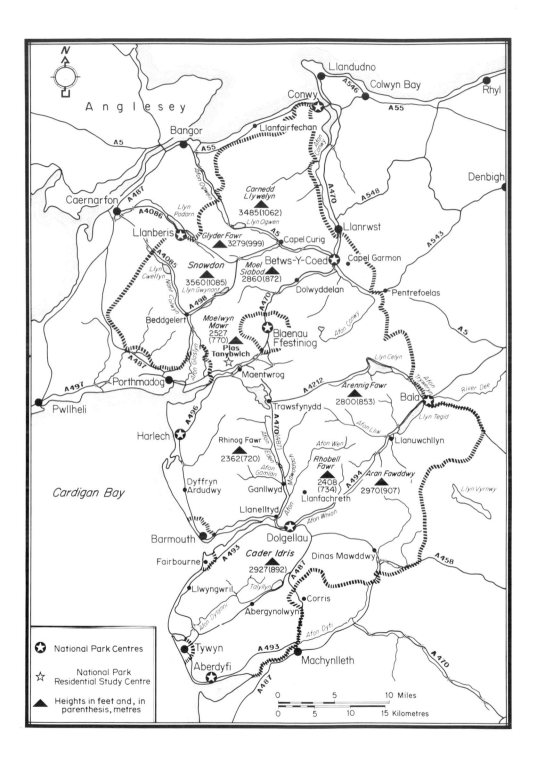

N

Llandudno

Colwyn Bay

Rhyl

Conwy

A546

A55

Anglesey

Bangor

A5

A55

Llanfairfechan

Afon Conwy

Denbigh

A548

A470

Caernarfon

A487

Carnedd Llywelyn

3485(1062)

A543

Llyn Padarn

A4086

A4085

Llanberis

Glyder Fawr

3279(999)

Llyn Ogwen

Capel Curig

A5

Llanrwst

Capel Garmon

Llyn Cwellyn

Snowdon

Moel Siabod

Betws-Y-Coed

3560(1085)

Nant Conwy

2860(872)

Dolwyddelan

Pentrefoelas

A498

Llyn Gwynant

A5

Beddgelert

Moelwyn Mawr

2527 (770)

A470

Afon Conwy

Plas Tanybwlch

Blaenau Ffestiniog

Llyn Celyn

A487

Afon Glaslyn

Maentwrog

Afon Tryweryn

River Dee

Porthmadog

A497

Arennig Fawr

Bala

Trawsfynydd

2800(853)

A496

A4212

Llyn Tegid

Pwllheli

Afon Lliw

Llanuwchllyn

Harlech

A470(487)

Rhinog Fawr

Afon Wen

2362(720)

Afon Eden

Rhobell Fawr

Aran Fawddwy

Llyn Vyrnwy

Afon Gamlan

2408 (734)

A494

2970(907)

Cardigan Bay

Dyffryn Ardudwy

Ganllwyd

Mawddach

Llanfachreth

Llanelltyd

Afon Wnion

Barmouth

Afon Eden

Dolgellau

A493

Dinas Mawddwy

A458

Fairbourne

Cader Idris

A487

A470

2927(892)

Llwyngwril

Talyllyn

Corris

Afon Dysynni

Abergynolwyn

Afon Dyfi

Tywyn

A493

Machynlleth

A470

Aberdyfi

A487

0   5   10 Miles

0   5   10   15 Kilometres

National Park Centres

National Park Residential Study Centre

Heights in feet and, in parenthesis, metres

10

mountains. To your north-east, beyond the deep trench of Nant Ffrancon, the ridge of the Carneddau runs away in a line of lofty summits not ending till they fall away seawards near Conwy. To your south-east, across another great gulf, rises a shapely and much-loved height called Moel Siabod. And if you turn south-west you see, intimately near, the craggy shoulders of 'Snowdon and his sons', to use a phrase from the most eminent of all those who have described these mountains, Thomas Pennant. But though only 3 miles distant (for a peregrine) Snowdon is attainable from Glyder by the earth-bound only after a challenging five-hour walk. For between these exalted heights lies the Pass of Llanberis, the wildest, deepest and craggiest defile in the whole of Wales.

In your walking, scrambling and perhaps breathless ascent of Glyder Fawr you have seen how the mountains build up as one huge terrace tiered above another; how they are slowly crumbling before your eyes; and how companionably they are grouped together to give the illusion of a much vaster range. From the summit you have looked far to the south and seen the long, gaunt scarp of Cader Idris as well as a crowd of lesser hills that peep at you over each other's shoulders. True, you have not looked at all the mountains and have seen nothing of the countless valleys and little side-dingles hidden among all those rolling ridges. But you have been able to grasp the quintessence of this wonderful corner of Britain and to accept that these beautiful hills and vales are a priceless bequest from some far-off eternity, a place of rare splendour which, by declaring it a National Park, we have resolved to pass on as unblemished as possible.

Early visitors

Ever since the mid-eighteenth century, people have been climbing Snowdon for the fun of it. Though by no means the first, the most famous of the pioneers was Thomas Pennant of Flintshire. On one of his visits he made it to the top by walking up from the west side after midnight. The weather was set fair, every star was brightly in its place and he reached the summit just as dawn came flooding across the uplands. He saw the rising sun fling the mountain's huge shadow many miles across the landscape and the views all round were vast.

Others before Pennant had written up their tours of Snowdonia but it was Pennant's engaging account (published in 1781) that caught the public's imagination and really put Snowdon on the tourist map. After him more and more people, mostly from England, felt moved to come and conquer this highest British peak south of the Scottish Grampians. They were quite happy to rough it for a few weeks while they not only climbed Snowdon but also admired the lakes, wondered at the water-falls and inspected the antiquities of a large part of north Wales. We should respect their toughness and resolve. They may have crossed England in a horse-drawn carriage but they were still nowhere near Snowdonia when the dreadful state of the roads, or the total absence of roads, forced them to take to horseback or their own two feet. They then had to face the prospect of spending the night in any old wayside hovel willing to open its doors. For at that time there were practically no hotels deep in the Welsh countryside and none at all in the uplands.

By the 1790s the tourists were becoming an accepted part of the scene. And they were very literary. Book after book came out describing their journeys, dissecting the scenery and pouring out their Romantic emotions and philosophisings. Much of what they wrote would not inspire us today but their contemporaries must have loved it, judging by the ever-rising tide of visitors. Then quite suddenly the roads improved. Telford's new Shrewsbury to Holyhead route (now the A5) was completed by 1830, the most novel and enterprising section being that from Betws-y-coed to Capel Curig and Ogwen and down Nant Ffrancon. This was soon followed by the Capel Curig to Pen-y-gwryd road which then went over Pen-y-pass and down to Llanberis with a branch from Pen-y-gwryd down Nant Gwynant to Beddgelert.

With the roads came the hotels and by the 1840s travellers could not only come right to the foot of Snowdon by carriage, they could also find decent accommodation. By now there were even guides waiting at the hotels to lead you to the summit. And if you rode up, there were atten-dants who came three-quarters of the way with you to keep an eye on your pony while you completed the rocky last part of the climb on foot. When Pennant got to the top in 1773 the only protection against wind and weather was a ring of piled up stones, no doubt the wreckage of an ancient cairn, and inside that circle people sat and ate their lunch. By the 1840s there was a crude building to shelter in and even refresh-ments on offer.

The road improvements made by Telford, Macadam and others pro-duced a travel revolution that was mainly of benefit to the well-to-do and those on business such as the many civil servants who, since the act of 1800 uniting Ireland with Great Britain, needed to get from London to Dublin. The new road through Nant Ffrancon saved them 20 miles compared with going via Chester and Conwy. It also showed them the beauties of Snowdonia and greatly added to its popularity.

Then around mid-century the railways got to north-west Wales, the Cambrian coast line via Barmouth to Pwllheli and the north coast route via Conwy to Holyhead. The age of popular travel had begun and every summer brought more and more visitors to Snowdonia, their numbers added to in the 1890s following the invention of the safety bicycle. 1896 brought what was literally the crowning achievement of the age of steam when railway engines began thumping their way up to the peak of Snowdon. For better or for worse (or both) the mountain has never been the same since.

A park is born

What is Snowdonia in terms of the use that people make of it? The answer best supported by tradition is that of the farmer: Snowdonia is essentially a pasture land for huge numbers of sheep and a smaller population of cattle. But this century the supremacy of the upland sheep has been challenged by the foresters. Their argument is that the country needs timber as well as sheep and that high moorlands can be used more economically for softwood production than for any other purpose. So since World War I extensive areas of Snowdonia have been vanishing under a blanket of conifers, and the process is continuing. Then alongside the claims of farmers and foresters a third voice says: nine-tenths of the people of Britain have to live in towns and they need open spaces where they can occasionally come and enjoy the tonic of wildness. It was in response to this voice that the National Park was created.

And where better? Here was a delightful part of Britain where tourists had long been made welcome, where even in the lowlands the population was small and where, on the higher ground, there were many leagues of almost uninhabited semi-wilderness. Granted this was a far cry from those real wildernesses that had been made into National Parks in the United States but it was as good as could be hoped for in as small and highly industrialised a country as Britain.

It was in the 1950s, after long years of discussion and argument, that Britain's National Parks were created, Snowdonia (1951) being one of the first. Occupying 838 square miles in the county of Gwynedd and second only to the Lake District Park in size, its boundary was drawn to exclude several coastal towns as well as Blaenau Ffestiniog in the centre. The Park is diamond-shaped. Its northern tip is a sea-breezy height called Mynydd y Dref which looks down on Conwy with its medieval town walls and castle, and across the bay to the Great Orme at Llandudno. From here it is 50 miles to the Park's southernmost corner at Aberdyfi which, like Conwy, is a charming rivermouth place lively with yachts and holidaymakers. From west to east the Park is narrower: Harlech with its commanding, seaward-looking castle, is 35 miles from the inland market town of Bala at the end of its beautiful lake. Strictly speaking, the only coastal area within the Park is the 20 miles of shore along Cardigan Bay, the north Wales coast being narrowly excluded. But for most of us the details of Park boundaries have little significance and no doubt the majority of visitors to the coast between Bangor and Conwy would be surprised to learn they are outside the National Park.

The highest peaks are all in the far north of the Park. Apart from Snowdon there are thirteen others over 3,000ft (915m), all of them north or north-east of Snowdon, the furthest off being Foel Fras at the other end of the Carneddau. To climb to any one of these high summits is for most of us the expedition of a whole day. Yet they are so compactly grouped (it is only ten crow miles from Snowdon to Foel Fras) that if you are fit enough and plan the trip well enough you can walk the whole fourteen in one very long day. And super-athletes can run them all in just a few hours.

The lesser peaks are scattered through all the Park, some of them crowned by such rugged tops and hollowed by such corries and naked crags that they look every bit as self-assured as Tryfan or Glyder Fawr. Close to Snowdon in the west are Mynydd Mawr, Moel Hebog and their many sister heights, all of them just the hills for a good day's scramble with the family. A little south rise Cnicht, Moelwyn and Manod, each to be cherished for its distinctive personality. Far away in the south-east is Arennig which from all directions seems to raise its double head above the surrounding country. Beyond Arennig the long, high crest of Aran is a dark-blue bar against the sky. And bathed in the sea winds of the west is the climbing and plunging north-south ridge of Rhinog which looks across a fair estuary to the shadowed face of Cader Idris.

If Snowdonia were one continuous high plateau it might well be a very dull place. So we can be thankful for the long ages of erosion which have so effectively carved up the landscape into the present pattern of lonely summits and intervening valleys. It is the valleys that have created the mountains and it is the valleys that play the major part in Snowdonia's general charm. For the Romantic visitors the valleys were everything. They lavished more praise, for instance, on the Vale of Ffestiniog than anywhere else in north Wales. For many of them a mountain was something they reluctantly climbed to give themselves better views of the lowlands. The uplands they found drab, depressing desolations because they were uninhabited and unimproved by agriculture. But the valleys they adored for their green fertility and their miles of billowing oakwoods.

Since then the world has changed. Urbanisation has spread hugely across parts of the British scene and today we see all our mountains and moorlands as precious oases where we can seek refreshment of spirit again and again. But there is much to be said for variety in life and this is to be found throughout the Park in its lakes, streams, woods, farms, shores, nature reserves, castles and churches, ancient and industrial monuments, narrow-gauge railways, villages, its holiday and market towns; and in getting to know its people.

The name 'Snowdonia'

People have sometimes objected to the name Snowdonia on the grounds that it has a vulgar, modern look about it, as if it had just been thought up by some tourist board. But in fact we learn in Camden's *Britannia* (1584) that it goes far back into the Middle Ages when legal documents were commonly in Latin. So when they wrote of Snowdon they automatically Latinised it to Snowdonia (or rather Snaudunia since the mountain was then called Snaudun). In past times Snowdonia has been a rather vague term. For many it has meant only the Snowdon–Glyder-Carneddau massif. For others it went much wider to embrace all the uplands of what until 1974 was Caernarvonshire, including the Lleyn Peninsula right along to Bardsey Island. Then suddenly, with the creation of the Park, the name took on a precise new meaning. In the west the Lleyn Peninsula was most regrettably excluded; but in the south, right down to the Dyfi river, whole districts which had always regarded themselves as remote from Snowdonia, now found themselves a part of the Snowdonia National Park.

The Park's name in Welsh is Parc Cenedlaethol Eryri. And with *Eryri* we are faced with etymological uncertainties. Does *Eryri* come from *eryr*? If so, it means 'the land of eagles'. Or is it from *eira* and therefore means 'the land of snow'? Or is it linked very far back with the Latin *orior* (to rise) which might suggest it means 'the land of mountains'? As all three derivations have their learned champions we are left free to choose whichever takes our fancy.

The weather

For Snowdonia's reputation for rain there is some justification. Even on the coast the annual rainfall is two or three times greater than that of London. On the mountains it is very much more and the travelogues of the early tourists are full of summer drenchings. But this is largely due to the unfortunate fact that August, the height of the visitor season, is quite often one of the wetter months. And with the hills rising so sharply from the coast the rainfall increases phenomenally as you go inland. What is drizzle at sea level can be a real soaker at 3,000ft (900m). Snowdon itself is a prodigious producer of rain (four times as much as on the nearby coast). The prevailing mild westerlies off the Atlantic often arrive heavy with vapour and condense into rain when they encounter the cold upper airs of Snowdon. With an average of 200in (5,080mm) of rain a year, Snowdon is one of the wettest spots in the British Isles, a distinction it shares with one locality in the Lake District and two in the Scottish Highlands. In some years its rainfall has exceeded 245in (6,223mm). All this precipitation may be depressing for lizards and other sun-worshippers but is heavenly for waterfall-watchers, some of whom will plod through the rain for miles to see a fall in its wildest rage. Such weather-braving devotion is essential because once the rain gives over the streams are very quick to go back to normal.

May is on average Snowdonia's driest month and even absolute droughts are not unknown in spring and summer. But fine weather is no guarantee of good visibility. Anticyclones can often bring sunshine but it may well be sunshine hazed over by east wind murk and on days like that you might as well leave your camera at home. The best hope of seeing vast distances from the mountain tops is to seize that sunny day or those few sunny hours which the sportive gods so often tease us with between Atlantic depressions. Typically the wind veers quickly from south-west to north-west, the clouds unravel, the sky is suddenly blue and out comes the sun with sparkling clarity. There may be frequent showers but there will also be many bright spells with big, white, shining clouds and then even photographers are happy. In winter those brave souls who face the frosts of the summits are occasionally rewarded with exceptional visibility when the valleys are deep in gloom.

In a typical winter in lowland Snowdonia we get a few cold days alternating with a few mild days and snowfall is usually slight. Inland, especially on the mountains, the picture is different. If it is raining heavily on the coast with the temperature just above freezing, it will be

16

The immediate view south-east from Snowdon's summit is across Bwlch y Saethau ('the pass of the arrows') to the ridge of Lliwedd whose east-facing cliffs are here in deep shadow. The Watkin path comes up from the right to join the Horseshoe track

slceting on the nearby hills and snowing hard on the mountains. Next day the tops will be white and may remain so for a week or two. But Snowdon, despite its greater height, finds its snow melting in the sea winds more quickly than the snow that lies farther inland on Aran Fawddwy or Berwyn. So Snowdon's skiers need to be quick off the mark as soon as the snow has fallen.

In very hard winters mountain conditions can be extremely severe and even the sea-shore can freeze deep down, killing shellfish and starfish in millions, as happened on the Cardigan Bay coast in January 1963. The blizzards of February 1947 filled mountain hollows with immense depths of drifted snow which turned to ice under its own weight and lasted for months; and on the north-east face of Carnedd Llywelyn in 1951 a deep gully kept its ice until the last day of July.

High winds often roar over Snowdonia and for every gale on the coast there are six or seven on the summits. Sudden squalls are frequent and are a special danger to people on cliff tops and knife-edges. In corries the gusts often blow from unexpected directions, sometimes rushing straight up instead of down the slopes and snatching at you with frightening power. Wind even troubles the Snowdon trains as they come up out of the Clogwyn cutting and expose themselves to the tempests that go howling up Cwm Brwynog. But for all of us the worst gales are those that bring blizzards and drifting snow. Then we should get down into the valleys without any further heroics and avoid bringing out the rescue teams.

Mountain mists are often tricky and dense fogs can be truly hazardous in precipice country. Even the local shepherds sometimes get quite disorientated and certainly every rambler should be equipped with map and compass. Yet even mists have had their devotees, like this tourist in 1774:

> During our abode amid those superb mountains, neither sun nor stars appeared for several days and, wrapt in an impenetrable mist, we were perpetually enveloped in a twilight obscurity. Our situation was like a scene of enchantment, impressing a superstitious ecstasy on our senses . . ..

Park problems

The creation of a National Park brings difficulties anywhere in the world but these are especially acute in a country like Britain where most land is privately owned and remains so though included in a National Park. So in British parks the landowners have a very large say in the matter of public access. Mercifully there is in Snowdonia a rich and precious network of public footpaths which we have inherited from the past, rights of way that originated as links between communities or were merchants' routes, miners' tracks, drovers' roads and the like. A few old paths have never been anything other than tourist tracks like those up Snowdon and other mountains. To some peaks what are known as courtesy footpaths have been agreed by the landowners. But to other summits there are tracks which, though much frequented, you will not find marked on any map because they are not yet formally recognised. Inevitably some paths, official or not, can be a cause of conflict between farmers and ramblers. Gates may be left open, allowing animals to stray; fences and walls may be damaged by those who wander off the footpaths; and, worst of all, sheep may be attacked by visitors' dogs. There is a clear obligation on us all to stick to the Country Code.

Quite different arguments arise from the threats of heavy industry. When our National Parks were being conceived people read the Hobhouse Report (1947) in which the basic philosophy was outlined and they noted that in the parks 'the characteristic landscape beauty is strictly preserved'. From this many of us reasonably concluded that henceforth the parks were secure against all encroachments of heavy industry. Nothing could have been further from the truth. The Snowdonia National Park had not long been in existence when, of all things, a nuclear power-station was allowed right in its centre. Then in 1972 an area near Dolgellau narrowly escaped being exploited for opencast copper mining and even the incomparable Mawddach estuary came near to being dredged for gold. The Park authority was quite powerless to resist these schemes because the Secretary of State for Wales had given the go-ahead for exploratory work. In the event these projects came to nothing because the speculators decided to withdraw. And while conservationists claimed this as a victory, the mining company said the decision was purely economic. Since then two gold mines have re-opened near Dolgellau and though it is true that they are so far very small, the fact that they are operating at all must raise the wider question: once the door is opened, against whom will it ever be closed?

The pros and cons of conifers are another lively issue. Besides many smaller plantations the Forestry Commission has four major blocks of trees in or on the border of the Park. They are near Beddgelert, Betws-y-coed, Dolgellau and Machynlleth. In addition there are extensive private plantations that are ever increasing. Some people find these new forests acceptable. Others strongly resent them as unbeautiful intrusions into the moorland landscape. Ramblers particularly dislike them because they find them dark and depressing to walk through, so closely packed are the trees. And they deplore the excessive use of alien species such as the Sitka spruce, the tree most commonly planted and which contributes most of all to the general gloom. Some naturalists concede that there may be a case for afforestation, recognising that if the Park were left to Mother Nature it would be covered with native trees up to nearly 2,000ft (610m). So they would like to see quite different forests being created, varied with many native trees which would be much more acceptable to wildlife than spruces and hemlocks.

Over the years the state forests have not enjoyed a good press and to improve its image the Forestry Commission has gone to much trouble and expense to welcome the public into the plantations by providing picnic sites and car parks as well as facilities for orienteering and car rallies. Thousands have enjoyed the first-class camp-site near

The much-climbed precipices of Lliwedd from across Llyn Llydaw. The summit ridge, a knife edge, is part of the Snowdon Horseshoe. The summit of Snowdon is off the picture to the right

Beddgelert; and the excellent visitor centre at Maesgwm in Coed y Brenin is, by its display and literature, highly informative about forestry, natural history and other countryside matters. There have also been modifications in forest practice to make the plantations a little more welcoming to native plants and animals. Unfortunately the mass use of spruces is still rife wherever large-scale planting takes place.

A possible threat to any very popular National Park is that of too many visitors. In Snowdonia the extreme case of overcrowding is Snowdon itself, Britain's most climbed mountain, whose summit has been described in the past as 'Britain's highest slum', 'the most abused mountain in Europe' and 'God's gift to litter louts'. These criticisms were given much publicity and since then things have improved greatly, but no matter how much tidying up goes on the fact still remains that a huge number of people may arrive together on this sharp peak in the middle part of a fine summer's day. In the 1920s those getting to the top were thought to be about 60,000 a year. In the 1950s the estimate was 100,000. Today it may be over a third of a million. Project these figures forward to early next century and they become truly horrifying. Perhaps a quarter of those reaching the top at present go up by train. The rest of us are hard at it wearing out paths that have to be maintained by heroic efforts and great expense.

As visitor numbers increase throughout the Park so does the demand for more hotels, chalets, camp-sites and caravans, more weekend cottages and houses for retirement, more car parks, petrol stations, roadside cafés and ice-cream vans, straighter and wider roads with copious lay-bys, rough tracks for car rallies and motor-bike scrambles, waters for angling, yachting, water-skiing and canoeing, and quieter spots suitable for birdwatching and field studies. Inevitably there are many clashes of interest and constant pressure for ever more development.

Sorting out all these problems is clearly a headache for someone and this leads us to the question: who runs Snowdonia? The answer is: a committee of Gwynedd County Council. Two-thirds of this committee are chosen from amongst elected members of the county council or a district council, and one-third are appointed by the Secretary of State for Wales. The committee sets the budgets, employs the staff and provides legal, financial, technical and administrative services. Responsible for the day-to-day running of the Park is the National Park Officer at Penrhyndeudraeth, he and his staff being concerned with planning, administration, estate management, conservation, information and wardening. The Park is financed 75 per cent by central government, 25 per cent by local government.

The National Trust

Apart from the Park officials, two major conservation bodies are very active in the Park. These are the Nature Conservancy Council, whose work is described in Chapter 4, and the National Trust, which has had a long and honourable association with Snowdonia, the first property it acquired anywhere in Britain being a few acres of hillside above Barmouth. Since that humble beginning in 1895 the Trust has risen to great importance and now owns 9 per cent – 47,000 acres (19,021 hectares) – of the Park, which makes it the second largest landowner after the Forestry Commission who hold 15 per cent. The aims of the National Trust are very much in line with those of the Park: to conserve the Park's natural beauty, to facilitate open-air recreation and the appreciation of nature, and to safeguard the economic and social well-being of those who live and work in the Park. The Trust owns many widely scattered properties including such celebrated spots as Aberglaslyn Pass; Dolmelynllyn (and Rhaeadr Ddu waterfall) at Ganllwyd; oakwoods in the Vale of Ffestiniog; Y Llethr (highest summit of the Rhinog range); Cregennen Lakes with part of Cader Idris; and Tal-y-braich, an area of mountain slopes near Capel Curig. But the most prestigious National Trust possessions within the Park are the two great estates of Ysbyty and the Carneddau.

The Ysbyty estate, which lies just south of Betws-y-coed, consists of 25,820 acres (10,460 hectares). Much of it is on the uplands and includes the great peat moor of Migneint; and there are also lowland farms and woodlands. The Carneddau holding not only embraces some famous mountains between the Conwy and Nant Ffrancon but also much of the southern Glyder range as well, including Cwm Idwal. On all lands held by the National Trust we can expect that the standard of farms and buildings will be high; and that farming and forestry methods will be compatible with wildlife conservation, as for instance near Ysbyty Ifan where some fine old herb-rich meadows are carefully maintained. The Trust works closely with the National Park Authority in giving access to its properties and looking after footpaths. It is also deeply involved in nature conservation as the owner of four National Nature Reserves and five Sites of Special Scientific Interest, all within the Park.

In coming to Snowdonia you have come to a beautiful land (though it is not without its scars). But there is much more to it than scenic splendour and many visitors gain vast satisfaction from getting to know about the Park's topography, the rocks, the world of nature, ancient monuments, history, architecture or the farming and social scene. One quality of Snowdonia is unmistakable: its Welshness. And when you hear Welsh being spoken you will be listening to a language that had been heard here for maybe a thousand years before a word of English was ever heard in Britain. You may not aspire to be a Welsh speaker yourself. But it will certainly add to the interest of your visit if you learn the meaning and pronunciation of those place-name elements – *pen*, *tal*, *llan*, *cae*, *bont* and so on – that are repeated all over the maps and are often so descriptive (see Appendix 1).

May the sun shine for at least part of your stay. But if it does not, if it rains and goes on raining, don't be downhearted: there is plenty to see and do in the many little towns and villages. Bear in mind that it is the rain that has cut all the valleys and created the lovely scene; and that it is the rain which keeps Snowdonia so green and its air so dustless (and puts a natural bloom on so many of the ladies' complexions!). You will find that the sunny hours which come after the rain are infinitely more delightful than the ever-lasting sunshine of those parts of the world where you never see a cloud in the sky for months on end.

1
THE SHAPE OF THE LAND

I have now traversed one of the most wonderful parts of Britain . . . . The views are grand, picturesque and pleasing, exhibiting a rich variety both of the sublime and beautiful . . . pure, simple nature, wild and conspicuously sporting grotesque rocks, towering hills and extensive lakes whence the most limpid brooks and romantic streams roll their waters down the sides of mountains, meander in pleasing murmurs through the vales or fall in beautiful cascades over rocky weirs.

So wrote an enthusiastic visitor to north-west Wales in the eighteenth century, and although we no longer use such flowery language we still hold Snowdonia in just as warm an embrace as the early tourists did. We are no more successful than they were at defining the essence of Snowdonia's charm but we are far more able to explain how the landscape has been created and shaped.

Ancient rocks

An essential feature of Snowdonia's geology, as of much of the rest of highland Britain, is that its rocks are all extremely old. (Palaeozoic is the technical term.) To put Snowdonia's rocks into order of time you could hardly do better than to begin well outside the Park in the north-west. Draw a line on a geological map from Holyhead to Bala and, one after another, it will cross the ancient rock systems of which north-west Wales is built. If you made a journey along this line you would, as you

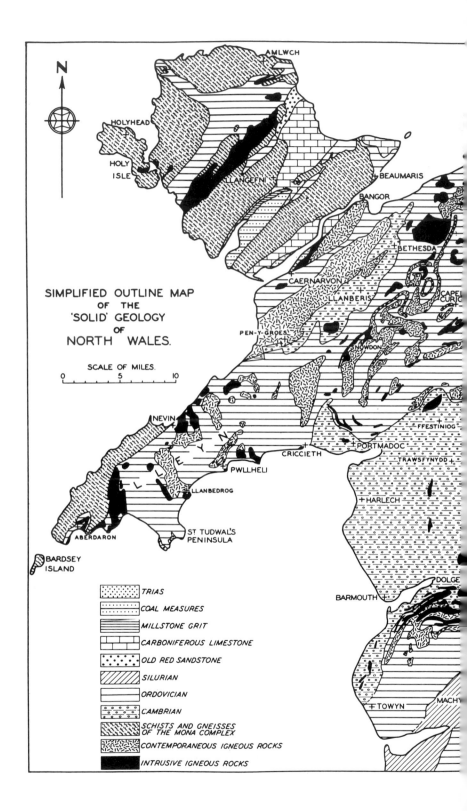

SIMPLIFIED OUTLINE MAP
OF THE
'SOLID' GEOLOGY
OF
NORTH WALES.

SCALE OF MILES.
0   5   10

N

AMLWCH
HOLYHEAD
HOLY
ISLE
LLANGEFNI
BEAUMARIS
BANGOR
BETHESDA
CAERNARVON
CAPEL
CURIG
LLANBERIS
PEN-Y-GROES
SNOWDON
FFESTINIOG
NEVIN
PORTMADOC
CRICCIETH
TRAWSFYNYDD
PWLLHELI
LLEYN
LLANBEDROG
HARLECH
ST TUDWAL'S
PENINSULA
ABERDARON
BARDSEY
ISLAND
DOLGE
BARMOUTH
TOWYN
MACHY

TRIAS
COAL MEASURES
MILLSTONE GRIT
CARBONIFEROUS LIMESTONE
OLD RED SANDSTONE
SILURIAN
ORDOVICIAN
CAMBRIAN
SCHISTS AND GNEISSES
OF THE MONA COMPLEX
CONTEMPORANEOUS IGNEOUS ROCKS
INTRUSIVE IGNEOUS ROCKS

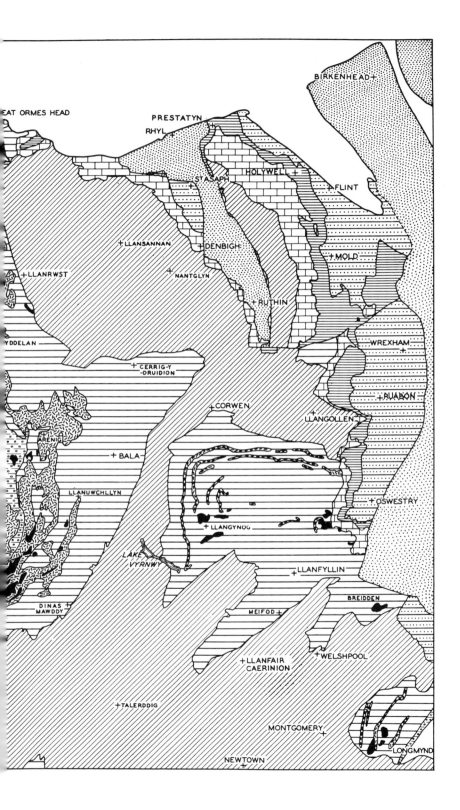

GREAT ORMES HEAD

PRESTATYN

RHYL

BIRKENHEAD+

HOLYWELL+

+STASAPH

FLINT+

+LLANSANNAN

DENBIGH+

+MOLD

+LLANRWST

NANTGLYN+

+RUTHIN

WREXHAM

YDDELAN

+CERRIG-Y
-DRUIDION

+RUABON

+CORWEN

LLANGOLLEN+

ARENIG

+BALA

+OSWESTRY

LLANUWCHLLYN

+LLANGYNOG

LAKE
VYRNWY

+LLANFYLLIN

DINAS+
MAWDDY

BREIDDEN

MEIFOD+

+WELSHPOOL

+LLANFAIR
CAERINION

+TALERDDIG

MONTGOMERY+

LONGMYND+

NEWTOWN+

crossed Anglesey, have some of the world's most venerable rocks beneath your feet – those of the Pre-Cambrian system, rocks that are almost without fossils because they were laid down in a world where life had scarcely begun. These same primordial rocks continue under the Menai Strait but after that you soon lose them under the rocks of the next era, the Cambrian, that rise high over Moel Eilio, Carnedd y Filiast and Elidir Fawr. Elidir's ridge is narrow and as you go on south-east you see from the map that you are very soon off the Cambrian rocks and on to those of the next age, the Ordovician, whose rocks include Snowdon, Glyder, the Carneddau and practically all the rest of the Park with the notable exception of the Rhinog country in the west which, like Elidir, is an outcrop of very hard Cambrian rocks.

From Elidir Fawr your south-east line passes near Glyder Fawr, then Moel Siabod, the Moelwyn hills, Manod Mawr and so over Arennig and down to Bala, on Ordovician rocks all the way. Carry on out of Wales and across Shropshire and you will gradually leave behind you all the really ancient rocks and find ever younger ones – Triassic, Jurassic and Cretaceous – as you cross the counties of Worcester, Warwick, Oxford and Buckingham and come at last to the Eocene clay on which London stands. On your journey you will have encountered as varied a range of the earth's rocks as you would find almost anywhere in the world in the same distance.

Snowdonia'a magnificent displays of naked rock inevitably excited the interest of the earliest geologists as they do of those of today, for there are still many unresolved problems. Some classic pioneer studies were made here last century and it was then that the names Cambrian, Ordovician and Silurian were invented, names that are now used throughout the world to describe rocks of the same age as those of north Wales, as indicated by the fossils they contain. 'Cambrian' comes from Cambria, a fancy name for Wales that was popular amongst Romantic and earlier writers. 'Ordovician' commemorates the Ordovices, a British tribe living in north Wales before and during the Roman period. The name has rather miraculously survived in the modern place-name Dinorwic (or Dinorwig), *din* being a fort and *orwic* meaning 'of the Ordovices'. 'Silurian' remembers the Silures, a tribe further south than the land of the Ordovices.

To begin to understand the geology of Snowdonia it is well to keep in mind that ocean and land have changed places more than once, perhaps many times, during the earth's long history. Great mountain ranges have pushed up out of the oceans, only to be slowly eroded away, their debris carried by the rivers and laid on the bed of the sea to form

The Pinnacles on Crib Goch seen from Cwm Glas-mawr. These jagged rocks are the most hazardous part of the Snowdon Horseshoe and should not be attempted in snow and ice except by properly equipped, experienced mountaineers

the stuff of future mountains. At the start of Cambrian times, 600 million years ago, what is now Snowdonia was a patch on the floor of an ocean. So it remained during the next 100 million years while a great depth of Cambrian rocks was deposited, the raw material coming from the decay of Pre-Cambrian mountains that were probably ranged north and south of the Cambrian ocean.

The details of what happened around the close of the Cambrian period need not concern us here. Suffice to say that after some hesitation the laying down of ocean-bed rocks went on through the 100 million years of Ordovician and Silurian time. But how could any ocean have found room for huge thicknesses of additional rock and still remain an ocean? What happened was that the trough (or geosyncline) in which the ocean lay went on sagging ever deeper into the earth's crust as more and more rocks were laid down on its bed, the result being that apart from rhythmic fluctuations, the depth of water remained fairly constant.

But a great change was coming. As the Silurian period gave place to the Devonian the ocean was at last pushed aside as land, including what is now Snowdonia, began to appear above the water, forced up by immense pressures operating through the earth's crust. As this new land appeared it was immediately assaulted by the forces of erosion. The Silurian rocks, being on top of the pile, were the first to be attacked and in the long course of time were swept almost entirely away. Then it became the turn of the Ordovician strata to be eroded. They too suffered enormous losses; yet even now, though they are only the worn-down stumps of yesterday's far greater peaks, they still stand up as mountains.

Ordovician volcanoes

Of the four ancient geological periods involved in Snowdonia's history it is the Ordovician that is of supreme importance, not only because its rocks occupy so much of the surface but also because it was a time of great, though intermittent, volcanic activity. While its sedimentary rocks were being laid down volcanoes were erupting on the ocean floor, spewing out lavas and ashes in vast quantities. There followed long quiet periods when further sediments deeply covered the volcanic rocks until the eruptions started again. And some volcanoes built up as huge cones whose fiery tops stood up as islands in the Ordovician sea.

This oscillation between calms and volcanic outbursts resulted in a complex alternation of sedimentary and volcanic rocks piled on top of each other all through the Ordovician system. And as well as the material poured or exploded out of volcanoes there were huge quantities of molten or gaseous matter which never erupted but was injected amongst the sedimentary rocks from below and cooled slowly to form the granites, felsites and dolerites which, exposed by erosion, now play a majestic part in the mountain scene. To add greatly to the complexity came those repeated phases of earth movement which rose to a crescendo soon after the Silurian period and which threw all this mish-mash of sedimentary and igneous rocks into a wonderful confusion of upfolds, downfolds and fractures whose interpretation still challenges geologists.

The Ordovician volcanoes were widespread, their general distribution today being boldly marked by the peaks of hard igneous rock which still stand high while softer rocks all round them have long since dissolved and gone down the rivers. An easy way of memorising the pattern of Snowdonia's former volcanoes is to think of them as a figure 5 with the top stroke missing (see opposite). You begin in the north at Foel Fras on the Carneddau. Then you come south-west by way of

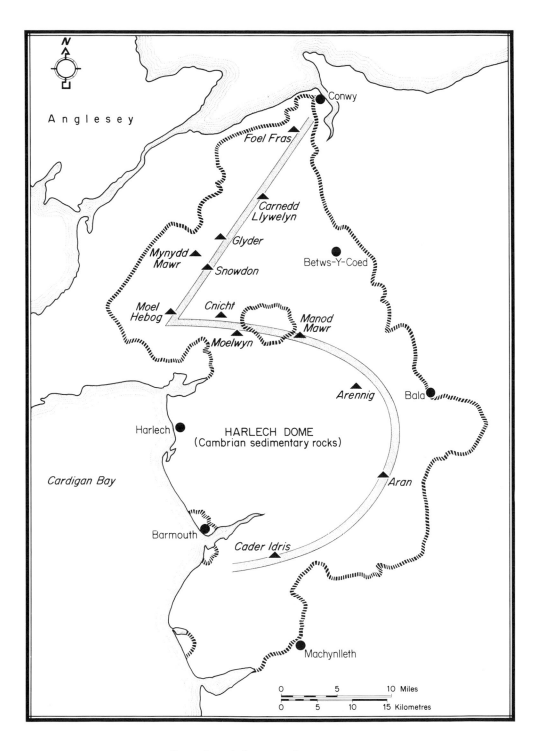

Snowdonia's former volcanoes

29

Carnedd Llywelyn and Carnedd Dafydd taking in Tryfan, Glyder, Siabod and the Snowdon group ending at Moel Hebog and neighbouring peaks. Then you turn east for Moelwyn, Manod and Arennig, come south to the Aran ridge and finally curve round westwards to Cader Idris.

It is one thing to talk about Snowdonia's ancient volcanoes and quite another to locate exactly where they erupted. The reason for this is that all their craters and cones have long, long ago been eroded away as thousands of feet of the Ordovician rocks have vanished. What we are left with are only the last remains of the lava fields and of the exploded matter that geologists know as the pyroclastic rocks. So it would be quite absurd to describe Snowdon as an extinct volcano as if it were some Vesuvius of only yesterday. For though Snowdon was born into a world of volcanoes and is largely their by-product, their craters were elsewhere.

Mountain making

The Devonian, which followed the Silurian period, was the age of Caledonian mountain building and is so called because it produced that striking design of parallel hills and valleys aligned north-east to south-west which is still so emphatically stamped on the face of Caledonia (ie Scotland) despite the wear and tear of 300 million years. In fact the geosyncline was not a merely British affair – it stretched all the way from Wales through Scotland to Scandinavia, the north-east to south-west line up of the ridges and vales being unmistakable

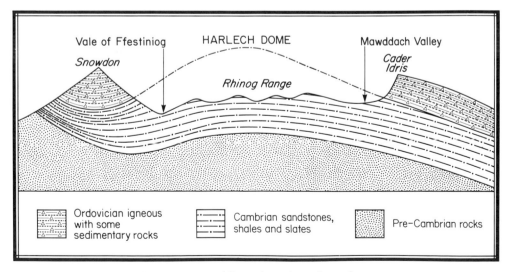

Basic pattern of Snowdonia's geological structure

The summit of Tryfan, one of Snowdonia's most popular peaks. It is scrambled to from all sides and there are many challenging climbs on its Ordovician lava cliffs. The view is from the slopes of Glyder Fach

throughout its length. The pressure needed to produce this pattern of folds is reckoned to have come through the earth's crust from the south-east, the rocks of Snowdonia being crumpled against the immovable block of Pre-Cambrian rocks in the region of Anglesey. Modern theories explain geosynclines and their related earth movements in terms of plate tectonics and shifting continents.

Syncline and dome

By the time this long process of distortion had subsided the block of rocks from which Snowdon was to be carved lay in the centre of a downfold in the strata. Rocks thus bent downwards into a trough (or syncline) are likely to get extra hardened by compression and this is probably why Snowdon has stood up to erosion better than all its neighbours. The down-curving rock beds of Snowdon, shaped like a pile of saucers, can sometimes be seen quite clearly on the east face when they are picked out by a sprinkling of snow. When we see these strata curving up out of the Snowdon syncline and obviously broken off at each end, we can easily project them skywards in our imagination. We then begin to get some idea of the immensity of the destruction which erosion has brought about (see page 30).

The detailed structure of Snowdonia is highly complex and at first sight the rock strata, nearly all steeply tilted, seem to slope this way and that in total disorder. Yet behind the chaos we can recognise a simple, basic pattern consisting of a trough in the north and a broad wave in the south lying alongside each other on a north-east to south-west alignment. The bottom of the trough runs through Moel Hebog, Snowdon, Glyder and the Carneddau. The top of the wave is midway between Moelwyn Mawr and Cader Idris, the whole wave, or arch, formation being known amongst geologists as the Harlech Dome because it is centred on the Rhinog range near Harlech.

The evidence for the trough, or syncline, that lies across the north of the Park is clear to see as you come up Nant Ffrancon from Bethesda to Ogwen on A5: across the valley on the flank of the Glyder range the strata are sloping (dipping as geologists say) towards the south, the way you are heading. They form the north side of the syncline which then curves round underground and reappears, now sloping upwards towards the south on Tryfan. But no sooner have we got beyond Tryfan than we find the beds arching over again and once more dipping towards the south on its neighbour Gallt-yr-ogof. This, however, is only a minor ripple, one of many in Snowdonia's profile, and does not affect the region's main structure. To see the rocks really climbing up the north side of the Harlech Dome we should take a look at Cnicht or the Moelwyn range. And as we would expect, the strata also rise boldly towards the south in many of the rocks at the north end of the Rhinog range, for there we are even more intimately involved with the Dome.

When we see these rock beds soaring upwards it requires no great strain on the imagination to picture them, hundreds of millions of years ago, following the dotted lines as sketched on page 30 and creating the great arch that curved over the country like a rainbow whose southern end came down to the Mawddach estuary and Cader Idris. It is in the cliffs of Cader's classic corrie, Cwm Cau, that you will best see the Harlech Dome's southward dipping strata. But they are also clearly visible on a smaller scale in the rocks alongside A496 on the north side of the estuary from Bont Ddu to Barmouth.

The view to Snowdon from eight miles south near Llanfrothen

Snowdon's rocks

Such is the geological diversity of Snowdonia that each summit stands apart as a distinct personality, not merely by external appearances but also by its internal composition and structure. Take Snowdon itself as an example, for it is a typical sandwich of sedimentary and volcanic materials. As you go up the track from Llanberis you first meet with the sedimentaries – the sandstones and slates, many of which have weathered to a rusty colour. Then, as the geologist F. J. North described it:

> . . . for about a quarter of a mile on either side of Halfway Station, there are darker slates, some of them blue-black. Beyond this, for half a mile or so, there are light-coloured massive rocks of volcanic origin, often flinty in appearance and in fracture. Still higher up, and for the last mile and a half, the route passes over more or less regularly arranged beds of which some are speckled greenish-grey rocks, rough to the feel and deep-brown on the weathered surfaces, while some are smooth and slaty. The rough-feeling speckly rocks are made up of fragments of lavas as fine as dust or as coarse as ashes . . . . In geological language rocks made up of fragmentary volcanic material are called tuffs when they consist principally of fine dust or contain particles large enough to be distinguished by the unaided eye . . . .

Though the top of Snowdon is a choice exhibit of this consolidated fine volcanic ash called tuff, this is not the whole of the story. For if you search immediately below the summit café you can find fragments of fossil shells (Brachiopods) which are rather like the cockles of today. So at the very apex of our highest mountain is a memory of life on a sea-bed of over 500 million years ago. It adds a touch of elegance to Snowdon's geology and we can be thankful that the summit so narrowly escaped being capped by the less interesting lavas of nearby Crib Goch.

Metals

Among the metals found in Snowdonia some have been commercially exploited – copper, lead, zinc, silver, gold, iron and manganese. Many

Looking up the Nantcol valley near Llanbedr to flat-topped Rhinog Fach. The rocks, of Cambrian age, are here near the centre of the Harlech Dome

Though normally breeding on sea cliffs, cormorants have long nested four miles inland on Craig yr Aderyn (Bird Rock) near Tywyn of their ores are the result of igneous activity and are materials of deep-seated origin that have risen through the earth's crust and reached the surface or nearly so. Frequently associated with fault lines, the metals have been forced up in hot liquid or gaseous form into cracks in the surrounding rocks where they have cooled and solidified. It is not surprising in an area like Snowdonia, which has seen so much igneous tumult, that there are countless metal-bearing veins. Along with their metals these veins, or lodes, often contain quartz and calcite, as can be seen in the spoil-heaps of mines. The amount of mineral in a vein varies greatly and unpredictably and mining has always been fitful and precarious (see Chapter 6).

Slate

So far we have looked only at sedimentary and igneous rocks but there is a third major class – the metamorphic rocks. These may have started out as igneous or sedimentaries but have since been so subjected to heat or pressure or both that they have been converted from one rock type to another. But although there are parts of Britain (north-west Scotland, for example) where such highly altered rocks are dominant in the mountain scenery, they play a lesser part in north Wales.

There is, however, one type of rock, produced by a mild degree of metamorphism, that is very important in Snowdonia and this is slate. The famous slates of Bethesda, Dinorwig and Nantlle were originally shales deposited in Cambrian times, and those of Ffestiniog and Corris were laid down in the Ordovician period. Then during the mountain-building era of Silurian and Devonian times, when immense sideways pressures rumpled the rocks into waves and troughs, these soft, fine-grained rocks were compressed and hardened into slate. During this process there was established the peculiar condition known as slaty cleavage. Sedimentary rocks normally split most easily along their bedding planes (or strata) but under great sideways pressure they may be so structurally altered that instead of cleaving as before they now split almost at right angles to the original beds and become slates.

Jointing

Distinct from but related to slaty cleavage is a type of splitting known as jointing. Through the many different strains to which rocks are subjected, a series of parallel cracks may develop, often at right angles to the bedding plane. Eventually these fissured rocks may shatter to form

Members of the Ramblers' Association on the north end of the Rhinog range. Here the Cambrian rocks have been split into blocks by the process called jointing

cliffs in which there are pillars and chimneys complete with those vertical faces so sought after by climbers; or they may split into blocks, sometimes of remarkably regular shape. Joints occur in all rock types whether of sedimentary or igneous origin and can sometimes easily be mistaken for strata.

Well-known effects of jointing are the Devil's Kitchen in Cwm Idwal and the Great Gully on Craig yr Ysfa. Jointing also accounts for the squarish columns in the cliffs of Glyder Fach and for the rectangular slabs of mountain-top detritus on the summit. The strikingly geometrical pillars of columnar basalt at the Giant's Causeway in Northern Ireland and on the Isle of Staffa in western Scotland are also the result of jointing. In Snowdonia such columns can be seen on a small scale on the slopes of Glyder Fawr above Llanberis Pass. They were first described by Snowdonia's earliest pioneer of geology, Edward Lhuyd, in 1691: 'One naked precipice is adorned with equidistant pillars, and these again slightly cross'd at certain joynts.'

Faults

The long torments of pressure which the rocks have had to endure have produced in the earth's crust a vast number of cracks, or faults, which have displaced the rock layers, forcing them out of alignment, up, down or sideways. Often the displacement is to be measured only in millimetres. But other faults are enormous enough to have produced spectacular scenic effects. Some fault-lines, being zones of weakness in the rocks, have been eroded to form valleys, the most striking example in Snowdonia being the deep trench that goes for 30 miles from Bala by way of the Talyllyn Pass to the coast at Tywyn.

Post-Silurian rocks

During the immensity of time since the end of the Silurian period, the Park's geological record is inevitably nebulous because there are no later rocks to tell us what has happened. It was long held by many geologists that Snowdonia had remained above sea level ever since Silurian days and that therefore no further rocks had been deposited. But there were others who believed in the probability that after the Silurian period Snowdonia was submerged, perhaps more than once, and that younger rocks such as the Triassic or the Cretaceous, had been laid down, only to be raised above sea level and totally removed by erosion.

In the late 1960s came convincing support for this second theory. The old assumption that the ancient Cambrian rocks of Rhinog must lie on the sea-bed of north Cardigan Bay was challenged by geologists who conducted seismic soundings there. Their results suggested a sea-bed of much younger rocks. So to settle the issue a very deep bore-hole was made at Mochras, near Llanbedr, as the furthest westward point of that part of the coast. This bore-hole proved the existence under Mochras not of Cambrian or any other very old rocks but of thousands of feet of rocks of the Triassic and Jurassic eras (180 million years ago). This means that underneath this part of the coast these huge thicknesses of younger rocks must be lying side by side with Cambrian rocks that are nearly 400 million years older than they are.

How can this be possible? The situation clearly points to a fault of huge dimensions. Along this fault line, which runs north-south close to the present coastline, the western part of the Harlech Dome's Cambrian rocks broke off and then slipped down for thousands of feet. So too did the Triassic and Jurassic rocks that lie on top of these Cambrian rocks. So now the younger rocks, not visible at the surface because buried beneath recent superficial deposits, are lying alongside the undisturbed section of the Harlech Dome. This fault is believed to have developed during Tertiary time (70 million years ago) and the strong implication is that the younger rocks once extended eastwards right over the Harlech Dome and probably over the whole of north Wales, so linking with the Triassic rocks of Cheshire. But, having so completely eroded away, they no longer play any part in Snowdonia's story.

The Ice Age

So we come to the threshold of our time – the last million years which, on the geological time-scale, is almost negligible. Yet its effects on the landscape have been enormous. Known as the Pleistocene period, it roughly corresponds to the Great Ice Age whose glaciers disappeared a mere ten thousand years ago. As these immense depths of ice, armed with rocks frozen into their undersides, made their slow way down from the mountains they smoothed the valleys from V-shapes into U-shapes. In the north, Nant Ffrancon, and in the south, Cwm Cywarch, are perfect examples of such glaciated valleys. But you will easily find others that are almost or quite as good. You will also see another major glacial feature – the hanging tributary valleys, a few with waterfalls dropping from them, that are so frequent along the sides of the major valleys.

Many corrie cliffs and knife-edge ridges as well as screes and other deserts of bare stones also show the work of glaciers. So too do the deep, moraine-edged lakes below the corrie cliffs. In fact practically every lake in the Park is a product of the Ice Age. Other obvious glacial effects are the many rocks perched incongruously about the landscape: they lie just where some glacier dumped them as it melted away. The ice has also left its mark by planing many rock surfaces and leaving scratch marks on them. (But beware of false interpretations: there are many scratch-like grooves on rocks that have nothing to do with glaciers.) There is an abundance of smoothed rocks in the shape of elongated hummocks which geologists call *roches moutonnées*: they too have been moulded by moving ice. A good example looks down Nant Ffrancon from the lip of Cwm Idwal. In fact if you want to find a site that exhibits the maximum amount of Ice Age evidence you will not find anywhere better than Cwm Idwal. In the south of the Park the same could be said of Cwm Cau on Cader Idris.

Boulder clay left behind by the ice sheets is also very widespread.

And south of Trawsfynydd there are a few of the long, narrow hillocks of clay called drumlins. At Moel Tryfan (SH 5156) near Nantlle, the Irish Sea ice, moving south from the Arctic, was forced up the hillsides to over 1,400ft (427m) where it deposited boulder clay and marine shells from the bed of the Irish Sea along with rocks it had carried down from Cumberland and Scotland.

A well-known coastal feature of the Ice Age is Mochras (or Shell Island) a prominent ridge of boulder clay which the sea is ever attacking, scattering its rocks and pebbles down the beach. And stretching out seawards under the water from near Mochras there are far more stones, some of them heaped up to form Sarn Badrig (St Patrick's Causeway), an extraordinary ridge of boulders that reaches seawards for a dozen or so miles and was a cause of many wrecks in the days of sailing ships. Like the similar but much shorter Sarn y Bwch near Tywyn and Sarn Cynfelin near Aberystwyth, Sarn Badrig is of uncertain origin but could well be a glacial side moraine. In the popular imagination it has long been regarded as the remains of a man-made sea-wall built long ago to protect an ancient low-lying kingdom now lost under the waters of Cardigan Bay. And although the idea of the Sarn being man-made is pure folk-lore invention there is behind the legend the undoubted fact that when the sea level rose as the Pleistocene ice sheets melted there was indeed a great flooding of coastal lands and forests and a drowning of all the nearby river valleys which are now estuaries very deep in silt.

Sarn Badrig can be seen clearly from the top of Moelfre, Diffwys and other Rhinog heights. It dries out for miles at very low spring tides but even at full tide it often divides the sea into two quite different zones of colour, sometimes pale-blue one side and a darker blue the other.

2
THE WORLD OF WILD FLOWERS

Much of Snowdonia's charm, apart from the beauty and grandeur of the scene, comes from the great variety of its wild, natural habitats. Purists may object that in reality very little of Snowdonia is truly wild and natural and this, in a strict sense, is true, for the ancient forests have long been cleared and almost the whole surface, right to the summits, has been modified by grazing. And even some of the precipices have been interfered with here and there by climbers deliberately clearing the vegetation off the rocks in a process they call 'gardening', a word that makes botanists shudder whenever they hear it in this context.

All the same, compared with so much of the rest of southern Britain, upland Snowdonia is still wild in the broad sense. For vivid proof of this you can, on any summer's day, go scrambling up the rocks and screes of the great corries under Snowdon or Glyder and find precisely those alpine plants in exactly the same localities where they were first excitedly reported by the pioneers of three centuries ago. And there they have flourished for maybe thousands of years while the natural world of the lowlands has been attacked and largely destroyed by the activities of restless mankind.

Alpine ecology

Anyone who takes the slightest notice of mountain plants can hardly fail to see that some rock faces are far richer in species than others.

Hard, dry rocks, for instance, are usually either plant-poor or, except for encrusting lichens, downright bare. In contrast, some of the best rocks for plants are those that are rotten and crumbling and therefore constantly forming new soils and releasing fresh supplies of mineral food. These soft rocks are also full of holes, cracks and ledges where plants can easily get in their roots. Crags made of this sort of rock (there needs to be constant water seeping down as well) can sometimes be picked out a mile away by the green luxuriance of their vegetation.

Chemistry also plays a vital part. There is a numerous group of alpine plants, some of them very rare, which are found only where the rocks yield calcium (lime). So the really superb, high-altitude botanical sites are where the rock is not only porous, fragile, wet and full of root-holds but also where lime is available. There need not be a great percentage of lime in the rock (far less than is found in true limestone is quite adequate) but it must be readily accessible to tiny rootlets. The best of these cliffs are those which face north or east and so escape the drying effects of summer sunshine and prevailing winds.

Lime, though elusive throughout Snowdonia, exists in both sedimentary and igneous rocks. In the sedimentaries it occurs, for instance, in what is known as the Bala Limestone, a rock that is by no means peculiar to Bala but goes far across the countryside in the form of rather rare, narrow bands. And sandwiched amongst the volcanic rocks on the great precipice of Clogwyn Du'r Arddu, is a band of sediments so calcium-rich that it has been described as a true lime-stone. Elsewhere in the Park some of the shales and mudstones are very locally calcareous judging by the wealth of their flora. But the general picture of the Park's sedimentary and metamorphic rocks, especially the grits and the slates that cover such large areas, is that they are lime-less and inhospitable to many plants.

It is the same with the igneous rocks. Most of them, whether they are the products of volcanic eruptions or have been intruded amongst the strata from below, yield a limeless soil. So the acid lavas such as form the rugged peaks of Tryfan and Crib Goch are largely bare of vegetation except for lime-hating plants such as heather and bilberry. It is the same with all the Park's granitic rocks such as those of Mynydd Mawr, part of Cader Idris and elsewhere. Not that all the igneous rocks are acid. A few of them, the pillow lavas on Cader Idris for example, are responsible for some of the most lime-blessed and flowery localities in all Snowdonia. And some intrusive rocks, like the dolerite that forms the great cliffs of Ysgolion Duon on Carnedd Dafydd, also yield enough lime to make most alpines happy.

42

But the most celebrated botanical sites on igneous rocks are those where well-stratified volcanic tuffs or ashes have been eroded to form crags looking north or east. They can be picked out on geological maps under the name Bedded Pyroclastic Series. The great east face of Snowdon that confronts you along the Pig Track; Cwm Glas-mawr above Llanberis Pass; the Devil's Kitchen cliffs in Cwm Idwal – these are famous examples of botanical meccas where the ledges are hanging gardens of alpine and other plants. No doubt the downfolded shape of the strata, such as you see on Snowdon and at the Devil's Kitchen, helps to concentrate a generous seeping of water on to those ledges.

Early plant-seekers

For so southern a British mountain, and one so close to the mild Atlantic, Snowdon is surprisingly rich in alpine plants. Or as Lewis's *Topographical Dictionary* (1833) rather quaintly puts it, 'Snowdon peculiarly abounds with that species of herbaceous plants called by Linnaeus *ethereae*, as being found only towards the summits of mountains'. Snowdon has the added distinction of being the first mountain in Britain to have been explored botanically. The year was 1639, the pioneer investigator, Thomas Johnson, a pharmacist from London. In the previous year Johnson had produced an edition of Gerard's famous *Herball* but here on Snowdon he was plant-seeking not for herbalism's sake but from pure love of botany. So, like his contemporary John Ray, the leading botanist of the time, Johnson stood at the threshold of the scientific age.

What, we may wonder, brought this enthusiast all the difficult and long way from London amid troubled political times to study the plants of Snowdon? Had he heard on some herbalists' grape-vine that the highest ledges of this far-off mountain were rich in strange plants? We shall probably never know, but what is certain is that he came with three others, that they climbed Snowdon on a wet day and yet managed to strike some of the best localities, as is shown by the astonishingly good list of plants they discovered.

Well before the end of the century three other botanists had followed in Johnson's footsteps: John Ray and Francis Willughby in 1658 and 1662; and, most celebrated of Welsh naturalists, Edward Lhuyd in the 1680s. So, a century before mountaineering began in Wales and two centuries before the arrival of the first rock climbers, botanists were groping their way up the highest crags of Snowdon.

It is fitting that what has been recognised as the first authentic rock climb in Wales is that of two ardent botanists, the Revs Bingley and Williams, in 1798. Though hampered by a basket carrying their food and their specimens, they somehow managed to get from bottom to top of the horrendous Clogwyn Du'r Arddu, one of Snowdon's highest and most nearly perpendicular cliffs. Not that they did the climb out of choice but, having got nearly half-way up what is now known as the Eastern Terrace, they found they could not get down and so just had to complete the climb or perish.

Summit flora

No doubt the early botanists included the very tops of the mountains in their quests but they would not have tarried long up there because the summit flora everywhere is extremely meagre. The gale-scourged peaks and ridges tend to be deserts of rock slabs and ruin, and where there is any vegetation it is often a monotonous grey spread of woolly-haired moss sheltering among the stones as best it can. Here and there you will see a wiry little plant called stiff sedge which is dedicated to summit life.

Not so much rare as hard to see is the dwarf willow, which really is a dwarf, often not reaching 2in (5cm). Yet a willow it truly is; it has woody twigs and tiny willow leaves, and in June or July shows yellow pussy flowers. Two clubmosses, the fir and the alpine, are freely scattered on these exposed places. A third, the stag's-horn clubmoss, does not get nearly so high on most mountains.

Corrie cliffs

The mountain plants dearest to the hearts of most botanists in Snowdonia belong to the group loosely known as the arctic-alpines, though not quite all of them are to be found both in the Arctic and the Alps. Most of them live in the cliffs just below the summits and are emphatically restricted to rocks that are rich in lime. Clearly the arctic-alpines are a relict flora made up of species that were among the tundra plants which crept into the lowlands of Britain from the Continent in the wake of the retreating ice sheets ten thousand years ago. Then as the climate went on getting milder the arctic-alpines could find acceptable conditions only on the mountains, and there they will presumably endure provided the climate remains as it more or less has been for the past two thousand years. Because Scotland's mountains are higher and more northerly there are more arctic-alpines up there than in Wales. In fact, Snowdonia is the southern British limit for a number of species; but a

The purple saxifrage, an arctic-alpine, is found only on lime-rich cliffs, making vivid splashes of colour in March and April, flowering even in icy conditions

few continue as far south as the uplands of Brecon and Glamorgan.

It may help towards a clearer picture of Snowdon's mountain cliff plants if we divide them into the abundant and the rare. Among the common ones the earliest to flower is the purple saxifrage whose mats of close-set bright-magenta flowers are a sudden joyous splash of colour even amid the icicles of late winter. Many weeks then follow before we see the white flowers of two other widespread saxifrages, the starry and the mossy, along with other treasures like alpine meadow-rue, lesser

Mountain sorrel is an abundant arctic-alpine in Snowdonia but is restricted to limy rocks except where it has colonised the lime-mortared walls of mine buildings as in Cwm Dyli

meadow-rue, moss campion, spring sandwort, mountain sorrel, alpine scurvy-grass and others. Thrift and sea campion, much better known as coastal plants, also flourish abundantly on the mountain cliffs. Two little ferns frequent on the lime-rich crags are brittle bladder fern and (more local) the green spleenwort.

Among the rare plants of the mountain ledges are alpine chickweed, arctic chickweed, hoary whitlowgrass, mountain avens, northern bedstraw, arctic saxifrage, alpine saw-wort, alpine cinquefoil, alpine bistort, alpine meadow-grass and a few others. All of them crowd together on the lime-rich cliffs and are totally absent from crags or indeed whole mountains whose rocks are limeless.

Snowdon lily

Snowdon's most distinguished arctic-alpine is undoubtedly the plant commonly but parochially called in Britain the Snowdon lily and known to science as *Lloydia serotina*, thus commemorating Edward Lhuyd (or Lloyd) who discovered it on 24 August 1682, a particularly creditable find because it was not then in flower. And when *Lloydia* is out of flower its grass-like leaves easily lose themselves among the neighbouring plants. This tiny white-flowered lily, no more than 4in (10cm) tall, has an extremely discontinuous distribution right round the northern hemisphere. Its nearest station east of Snowdon is 600 miles away in the Alps. Westwards you need to go all the way to the Rockies before you will find this little treasure. It is also in the Caucausus, the Carpathians, the Himalayas and Siberia but nearly everywhere is reported to be uncommon. Its peculiarity in the British Isles is that it grows only on or close to Snowdon, its absence from Scotland being especially strange. In Snowdonia it is said never to produce viable seed, multiplying by its bulbs producing offsets instead. Perhaps there is a link between this mode of reproduction and the fact that on Snowdon it finds itself living in a milder, damper climate than anywhere else in the world where it grows.

For many years the Snowdon lily has suffered terribly from being over-collected by botanists and gardeners attracted by its beauty, its rarity and the romance of its situation. So today, long ago robbed from accessible places, it grows mostly well out of reach and is best viewed through binoculars where it is visible on the highest ledges (but make sure you really are looking at *Lloydia* and not the very similar wood anemone that sometimes grows near it). Its chief flowering time is in late May and the first half of June. It grows here and there in small colonies on several lime-rich crags along a belt of uplands 7 miles long.

Fern rarities

If any plants have been collected more than the Snowdon lily it is the ferns. Especially in Victorian times the craze for collecting ferns brought people to Snowdonia in pursuit of rarities. The result is that three ferns, always very scarce, are now reduced almost to vanishing point: Killarney fern, alpine woodsia and oblong woodsia. Holly fern too was greatly reduced and is now almost as rare as these.

Today such plants are safeguarded by law and as some enjoy the additional protection of being in nature reserves the hope is that even now they can be saved from extinction. Perhaps some would benefit from the sort of help given to one of Snowdonia's rarest arctic-alpines, the tufted saxifrage. A few years ago seeds from the last few surviving plants were taken to botanical gardens which raised new plants that in turn produced many seedlings and these were then planted in the corrie from where the original stock came. So far this experiment has had encouraging results.

Other mountain plants

A surprise, if the mountain flora is new to you, will be to discover that jostling with the alpines for a place on their high ledges is a multitude of what we normally think of as lowland plants. Typical are wood-sorrel, wood anemone, water avens, devil's-bit scabious, wild angelica, common valerian, meadowsweet, common violet, primrose, globeflower, Welsh poppy, ox-eye daisy, slender St John's-wort and many others, including a few scarcer ones like early-purple orchid and grass of Parnassus. Clearly they all enjoy the summer coolness and dampness of fertile mountain cliffs which are turned away from the midday sun. No doubt many date back to a time when the uplands were partly covered with native trees.

High grasslands

No matter how precious our arctic-alpines may be, it is well to keep them in perspective. Their special crags occupy the merest fraction of the mountain scene and the plain truth is that most of the uplands are covered by grasslands which, though they make beautiful scenery, are of scant botanical interest except to a few specialists.

There are over three hundred species of grasses in the British Isles yet the whole spread of mountain turf is made up of very few of them. Where the drainage is good and the soil not too poor there is commonly the grass called sheep's fescue. Animals find this so nutritious that eventually they may so weaken it by over-grazing that it gives place to an aggressive and far less edible species called mat-grass which increasingly covers vast areas of the uplands. Where the drainage is bad you

Snowdon and neighbouring mountains are the only localities in Wales for the holly fern but even here it is rare and restricted to lime-yielding rocks. It was grievously over-collected during the nineteenth century fern craze

One of the rarest of Snowdonia's plants, the insectivorous great sundew, about four inches tall, grows in very acid conditions. Only in warm sunshine does it open its little white flowers

will often find slopes and hollows alike totally occupied by purple moor-grass whose big, lumpy tussocks, so pallid in winter, are extremely tiresome to walk or rather stumble across; or similar wet ground may be knee-deep in huge stretches of various kinds of rushes.

Peat moors

Heather moor, except in the Rhinog country, is not very widespread in Snowdonia and has greatly diminished everywhere (including Rhinog) this century under the combined attack of farming (burning and grazing) and forestry (ploughing and planting). This is a sad loss because large spreads of heather are essential to the survival of various desirable birds and insects. Often destroyed along with the heather moors are the peat bogs with their very interesting and specialised flora. Typical plants are round-leaved sundew, bog asphodel, bog bean, cotton grass, sphagnum mosses and various sedges. On lower moorlands where the climate is kinder and where the bog merges into less acid ground there may be many other attractive species such as marsh violet, marsh St John's-wort, petty whin, marsh cinquefoil, marsh speedwell, sneezewort, heath spotted orchid, lesser butterfly orchid and a wide range of sedges.

Very locally, where heather and bog mosses grow together, you may come upon a tiny orchid with reddish flowers and easily known by twin, round little leaves half-way up the stem: the lesser twayblade. You will probably need to part the heather to find it and you need keen eyes too because it is often quite hard to see growing out of clumps of reddish sphagnum moss. July is its best month but it can be found a little earlier or a lot later because its flowers are long lasting. It is best known in the northern half of the Rhinog range where heather is vastly abundant but it is also reported from Cader Idris and Arennig.

Water plants

Snowdonia's lakes and reservoirs – over a hundred and fifty of them if we count the smallest – vary much in altitude, depth, acidity and degree of exposure. Some are rock-bound and have gravelly floors; others are moorland tarns with squelchy margins. The deepest lakes, especially where mountain cliffs go straight down into the water, are

Barmouth, popular resort on Cardigan Bay, is squeezed between sea and mountain

the most lifeless because so few plants can live in their dark depths. Quite different are those which lie in shallow, stony basins. Under their clear water, or sometimes out on the margin of the pool, you can see carpets of lake-bed plants with rosettes of narrow leaves which may belong to any of five species, the commonest being shore-weed and water lobelia. The three others are awlwort and two kinds of quillwort. The long leaves of floating sweet-grass and floating bur-reed make elegant patterns on the surface of such lakes. To find waters rich in lilies, milfoils, starworts, crowfoots and pondweeds we need to seek the more fertile pools of the lowlands.

Nearly all the mountain torrents are poor in plants except aquatic mosses. They are too often scoured from source to sea by spates and can never hope to achieve the plant-richness of slow-moving lowland rivers. But special to many of the Park's streams are the deep, narrow gorges they have carved for themselves. Cool, shadowy and ever-damp from the splash and spray of falls and rapids, and perhaps in all history never interfered with by man, these ravines come as near to being totally natural as the mountain cliffs themselves. Mosses and liverworts abound in them; so do ferns, including such rarities as hay-scented buckler-fern, Tunbridge filmy-fern and (you never know your luck) perhaps even the Killarney fern.

Oakwoods

Five thousand years ago much of Snowdonia below the summits was still covered by broad-leaved trees. But since then these native forests have been almost entirely destroyed by a worsening of the climate and by the spread of farming. Today the only natural, or rather semi-natural, woodland consists of small, relict patches of sessile oak and birch, with ash, alder and a few others, typically strung out along hillsides. Such woods are scattered throughout the Park but are at their best in the Vale of Ffestiniog (see Chapter 4).

The soils of these woods are predominantly sour and among their commonest wildflowers are wood-sorrel, wood sage, slender St John's-wort, common cow-wheat, foxglove and sometimes sheets of bluebells. A slight lessening of acidity allows in a more varied flora including red campion, herb-robert, wood anemone, lesser celandine, ivy-leaved

The most widespread orchid in Snowdonia, the heath spotted orchid varies from almost white (its commonest colour) to deep lilac-rose

53

speedwell, wood speedwell, bugle, wild strawberry, enchanter's night-shade and others. But only very locally are the woodland soils lime-rich enough for flourishing populations of dog's-mercury, sanicle, woodruff, yellow archangel, moschatel, ramsons, wall lettuce, early-purple orchid, wood melick and false brome-grass. In autumn all the woods that are rich in leafmould are colourful with infinite numbers of toadstools, puffballs, fairy clubs, brackets and other fascinating products of the fungus world.

Bracken jungles

No doubt the primal forests had bracken as part of their undergrowth, and today, though the trees vanished long ago, many hill slopes are still densely covered by this fern that is so beautiful in autumn and winter when it reddens in the late afternoon sunshine. But though decorative, bracken occupies ground which could be turned to use as pasture land and farmers would love to get rid of it. The procedure is, however, so very costly, involving aerial spraying and ploughing, that there is as yet little sign of bracken disappearing from the landscape except very locally. As well as on treeless slopes, bracken is totally dominant in many woods, especially where the soil is deep, well drained and lime-free. In damper woods other ferns may riot, especially lady fern, male fern and broad buckler-fern.

The old meadows

Snowdonia's lowland and semi-upland meadows used to be rich in wildflowers before the coming of the modernisation programmes (drainage, ploughing and re-seeding) which have been so intensive in recent years. Nowadays you have to search quite hard to find any unimproved meadows with their old flora still intact. On most farms all you can now hope for is that some wild corner or unploughable field margin has been left untouched.

Among the typical plants of the more lime-rich meadows are bitter vetch, saw-wort, quaking grass, globeflower, twayblade, wood spotted orchid, fragrant orchid and greater butterfly orchid. Rarer species of such rich fields are grass of Parnassus, melancholy thistle, wood horse-tail, northern marsh orchid, frog orchid, small white orchid, moonwort and adder's-tongue. More acid meadows, sometimes yellow with buttercups, have a less varied flora. Among their more distinguished plants are petty whin, ivy-leaved bellflower, bog pimpernel, whorled caraway

Juniper is an attractive shrub found locally on acid rocks and block scree. In Snowdonia it grows prostrate over the rocks instead of in the upright form it has in some parts of Britain

and devil's-bit scabious. It is often worth while looking for the old meadow flora in churchyards or chapel graveyards because these may well be the only patches of ground for miles that have not been ploughed for ages.

Foreign shrubs

Two conspicuous alien shrubs excite admiration and curiosity among visitors to Snowdonia. One is willow-leaved spiraea which is abundant in hedges in the country between Bala and Ffestiniog. From June to August its sprays of pale-pink flowers are an adornment of many a roadside. It was widely planted by a Bala landowner in about 1870 to make hedges that would be good shelter for game birds. But it proved to have serious disadvantages: it spreads rapidly into the fields and has to be fought against year by year; and it is not strong enough to make a stock-proof hedge.

The other exotic shrub is rhododendron, which is much more widespread. It was originally planted for its beauty in gardens and as pheasant cover in woods but it has escaped into the countryside and is still advancing at an alarming rate. It begins as scattered bushes but these eventually merge into an impenetrable jungle, suffocating all smaller plants. Its purple-pink flowers are at their best in June and are spectacular when covering whole hillsides as at Dinas Mawddwy or Aberglaslyn Pass. All the same there are plans to get rid of it though the problem is a formidable one.

The seashore

Dunes with their sandy foreshores, several miles of cliffs, long stretches of shingle and some attractive estuaries and stream mouths – these make up the Park's seaboard on Cardigan Bay. The best of the dunes are protected as nature reserves and can be left to Chapter 4. The cliffs stretch south from near the Mawddach to the Dysynni. Nowhere are they high and everywhere they are fragile; in fact there are places where they are made of nothing harder than boulder clay. From spring to autumn they are colourful with wildflowers – sea campion, thrift, scurvy-grass, wild carrot, scentless mayweed, buck's-horn plantain, English stonecrop and many others. Three species – early-purple orchid, rock samphire and sea spleenwort – are very local on these cliffs.

The shingle of the beaches has its own special flora which is perhaps best developed on the broad spread of pebbles at the mouth of the Dysynni north of Tywyn. Typical shingle plants are yellow horned poppy with its long, slim, curving seed-pods; bird's-foot trefoil, kidney vetch, sea campion, sea sandwort and various oraches. Not quite on the shore but on waste ground close to it (at Aberdyfi and Barmouth for instance) you may see tall stands of fennel, elegant with yellow flowers and hair-like leaves.

Estuaries

The delightfully unspoilt estuaries are full of interest for naturalists. There are green swards of sea meadow-grass which are kept fertile by the spring tides that regularly cover them. Also common on the saltings are sea aster, sea milkwort, sea plantain, sea arrowgrass, annual sea-blite, parsley water dropwort, scurvy-grass and thrift. Locally the mud-flats have both annual and perennial glasswort. An extremely vigorous coloniser called cord-grass, introduced to the Dyfi in 1921 as a land-reclaimer, has long since spread round the coast to other estuaries and inlets and now occupies hundreds of acres. It is a worry to conservationists because it not only smothers glassworts and other plants but also obliterates the feeding grounds of wading birds. If you know the estuaries of eastern England you may at first wonder what is different about those of Snowdonia. It is the virtual absence here of those two abundant and attractive plants, sea wormwood and sea lavender.

Other notables

A few remaining plants of distinction can round off this sketch of Snowdonia's flora. One of the most remarkable is the hairy greenweed that is sparsely scattered high on the eastern end of the Cader Idris range, its peculiarity being that up there it manages to defy the mountain elements although elsewhere in Britain it seems to be a not very hardy species found only in mild places such as the cliffs of Cornwall or St David's Head in south-west Dyfed. Two other special plants of the hill country are not true alpines despite their names. Alpine enchanter's-nightshade is a rarity of lime-rich screes; and alpine penny-cress is a lowlander of the Conwy valley near Llanrwst.

An alien plant not usually thought of as an alpine has nevertheless managed to invade the alpine zone with astonishing success this century. Unknown in the Park before 1930, the New Zealand willowherb has been creeping about damp, stony places ever since, getting higher into the uplands year by year. It is a prostrate plant whose tiny round leaves and white flowers on delicate stalks you can now see in abundance on many of Snowdonia's mountains.

Another plant of much interest is the fragrant, white-flowered, fine-leaved umbellifer called spignel. It grows thinly scattered on the hill slopes between Dolgellau and Llanuwchllyn and is possibly a relic of the herbalism of the Middle Ages. Certainly its distribution is suggestive of historical associations for it grows along a Roman road, near a medieval trackway and not far from an ancient religious house. This mainly Scottish plant is not known further south in Britain than Cader Idris. In contrast the wavy St John's-wort, perhaps the loveliest of a very beautiful family, reaches no further north than a peat bog along the Mawddach estuary.

3
BIRDS, MAMMALS AND OTHER WILDLIFE

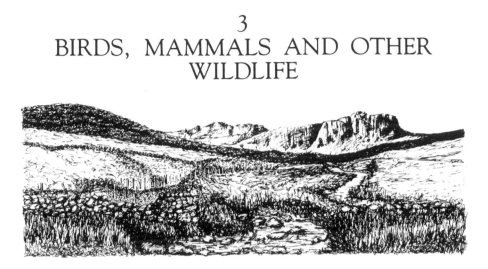

Variety, as we have seen in the last chapter, is the hallmark of Snowdonia – variety in altitude, aspect, rocks and soils and therefore vegetation. From the sands of the open shore through dunes, farmlands, wooded, brackeny or rocky valleys up to the high moors and summits there is an infinity of niches for wildlife, even though the Snowdonia we know today is a decidedly tamer place than the wild and forested region it was in the Dark Ages. Since those far-off days we have lost several splendid mammals and birds. Did the bear survive after the eighth century? At what remote day did the wolf, the boar and the beaver say goodbye? How long is it since bitterns, spoonbills and marsh harriers nested in Snowdonia's now vanished reedbeds? Certainly both red and roe deer seem to have gone about three centuries ago; so too the golden eagle. And perhaps the last to vanish (but the evidence is poor) was the wild cat, which may have survived into the nineteenth century though it seems no skin exists in any museum.

Despite these losses Snowdonia is still a refuge for some distinguished mammals and birds which were wiped out or sadly reduced by nineteenth-century gamekeepers and farmers over wide areas of southern Britain. The polecat, for instance, survives in some abundance and even the pine marten still holds on, though perhaps precariously. Ravens and buzzards are in good numbers; and peregrines, having recovered after a severe decline caused by agricultural pesticides in the 1960s, are once again well established. In these days of more enlightened attitudes to nature conservation, the hope is that these formerly persecuted species will go on holding their own or show an increase and that others such as the red kite, hen harrier and Montagu's harrier will one day be able to recolonise old haunts. And eventually why not the golden eagle?

Birds

When the Welsh historian and topographer, Nicholas Owen, climbed Snowdon in about 1790, he commented on the general scarcity of birds: 'I observed no birds in this region except the red kite and a little brown bird, sparrow-like, and the cormorant.' Clearly Owen was no bird expert but his point is a valid one: even in summer the mountain birds are nowhere abundant. In winter it can be far, far worse; then you can go for miles across the hills without seeing so much as a crow. The kite Owen saw (and evidently took for granted) was something he almost certainly would not see today anywhere near Snowdon because in the following century this large, elegant and once common raptor was wiped out by gamekeepers in Snowdonia and, although now legally protected, it has not yet made a come-back except very locally in the far south of the Park. Compared with his kite the cormorant on Owen's list was, from today's viewpoint, a much more routine occurrence: it had probably flown up from the coast for a round of the trout lakes, just as cormorants often still do. His little brown bird was presumably a meadow pipit which probably was then, as it is now, by far the commonest bird of the uplands.

A bird Owen might have met with, given a bit of luck, is the chough, assuming that there were choughs on the Snowdonian uplands in those days. Certainly they are there today, thinly scattered from the hills of Lleyn in the west to the Carneddau in the east as well as south all the way across the Park, nesting in natural rock crevices or, more often, in old mines and quarries. At a distance they can look like jackdaws but usually their distinctive call, a ringing *chee-ow*, identifies them. Close to, their red legs and curved red bills make them unmistakable. They live by picking grubs, small beetles and ants out of closely grazed mountain turf. The nesting pairs are well spaced out but soon after the breeding season you may find them in flocks of thirty or more. Most winters they go down to the unfrozen pastures of the lowlands. In very severe weather many die.

By strong tradition Snowdonia is linked with golden eagles and there is little reason to doubt that they were breeding here until about 1700.

Precisely where any eyrie was sited is not recorded, the nearest anyone comes to naming a locality being the botanist, Thomas Johnson, who said they were nesting on Carnedd Llywelyn when he came in 1639 and certainly there are fine eagle-worthy corries near this third highest British summit south of Scotland. Today the most distinguished occupants of the mountain crags are the peregrines which are thinly scattered throughout the Park, many breeding at sites that may well date back centuries. From some cliffs the birds have doubtless been driven away by rock climbers but on the other hand there have been instances of peregrines breeding successfully though very close to popular climbs.

Many of the Park's wilder precipices have their nesting pair of ravens. Their great stick nests, often in the shelter of an overhang, are typically on high ledges inaccessible to shepherds, who heartily detest all ravens and crows for pecking out the eyes of dying sheep. Early in March the ravens repair their nests, lining them warmly with wool, and by mid-May the young have already fledged and gone. Where ravens and peregrines are breeding near each other there is often trouble between them and spectacular aerial combats. This is a competition for territory but not for food. For while the peregrines prey largely on homing pigeons, the ravens (especially in winter) take much carrion mutton. An interesting question is what would happen to peregrines if pigeon-racing were to go out of fashion, or to ravens if sheep ceased to be pastured on the hills?

Something very like the ill-tempered bickering between peregrines and ravens can be seen on crags where kestrels are neighbours to carrion crows. There is the same mutual distrust and similar aerobatics as the kestrels dive like darts on the crows, always just missing them as a peregrine just misses a raven. Also breeding in the mountain cliffs there are buzzards, but only very few. For though you may see them fairly often floating and circling gracefully over the hills they are really much more at home down in the valley farmlands and oakwoods.

Add only two other birds – wren and ring ouzel – and the tally of regular mountain crag birds is complete. The wrens, so tiny in the vast surroundings of a corrie, would seldom be noticed if they did not advertise themselves by their song which is so startlingly loud and shrill when it suddenly bursts at you from close range amongst the rocks. The ouzels clearly like the cover of heather under which to hide their blackbird-like nests. They are elusive birds, fast on the wing and quickly out of sight into the next gully. Like the wrens they would hardly ever be noticed if it were not for their frequent song. This is a lovely wild note,

Carrion eaters. Many sheep may die when deep snow covers the hills, their flesh
becoming food for kite and raven or, as here, for buzzard and carrion crows

or rather four or five notes, all on one level. On a still day they carry far
down the slopes from high amongst the heathery terraces.

The long tumbles of stone, some loose underfoot, some in repose,
that are spread fan-shaped below the crags, have one special bird – the
wheatear. Often before the end of March it arrives from Africa, bringing a touch of life, song and colour to the sombre screes. You will find
it on the grassy moorlands too but only where there are rocks or walls
to sing from and to provide nesting cover. The wheatear, unevenly
scattered throughout Snowdonia, breeds all the way down to the coast
but it nowhere seems more at home than up in the real mountainy
places.

On the Park's highest and most spacious grasslands there is clearly room for vast numbers of skylarks and meadow pipits. But in fact these upper regions are far too windy, cool, sunless and wet to sustain enough small life to feed more than a handful of birds. So we need to come down to much lower moors to hear the tinkling songs of pipits all round us and plenty of lark song overhead. Still, there is one bird truly of the mountain tops – the dotterel, a creature so rare and inconspicuous that to meet with one is a once-in-a-lifetime experience. Yet this beautiful little plover probably comes every year on spring and autumn passage, feeding briefly at traditional calling places all the way across the roof of Snowdonia from the Carneddau to Cader Idris. On rare occasions it has nested high on the moors.

Wherever the grassland gives way to heather there are usually red grouse, though nowhere in the Park is this now a common bird. We can, however, console ourselves that the few grouse that survive are genuinely wild and unassisted by the armies of hawk-destroying game-keepers who maintained unnaturally high numbers of grouse until earlier this century. Especially where heather grows amongst rocks you could be lucky enough to meet with a pair of breeding merlins, but for unknown reasons this little falcon has greatly declined in recent years and is now a rarity. But not everything on the heather moors is loss. In recent years Snowdonia has acquired a new breeding bird, the twite, which has spread down from northern Britain. It is still very local and sparse but should be looked out for anywhere in the Park. Perhaps it is easiest to find in late summer when it bands into flocks to feed on thistles and other seed-producers.

Peat bogs, rushy pastures and wet, rough grasslands of the lower hills are the summer home of snipe, curlew and lapwing. But there seems to be nowhere in the Park where dunlin and golden plover breed regularly today as they did last century. Nor are nesting waterfowl anywhere common. The high tarns have a very few mallard and teal but many of these waters, being foodless, are virtually birdless except for an occasional colony of black-headed gulls. The gulls, however, only resort to the lakes for protection: for food they go elsewhere. It is only the more fertile lakes and pools of the lowlands which have breeding birds in any numbers – mostly mallard, moorhens and a few coots, mute swans and little grebes. Breeding great crested grebes are everywhere rare.

Where there are reeds or other tall poolside plants there are likely to be reed buntings and sedge warblers but the reed warbler, a recent new-comer, is still far from common. In winter, diving ducks and coots are numerous on some lowland fresh waters. The Park's many sparkling rivers and sidestreams are nesting places for dippers, grey wagtails and common sandpipers, all of them rather sparsely scattered from the uplands down to sea level. In contrast, the kingfisher is something of a rarity in the nesting season but in autumn and winter it is not uncommon along the estuaries. At no time of year is it a bird of the higher ground.

The huge modern conifer plantations, largely of Sitka spruce, are a mixed blessing to wildlife. The vegetation comes off worst because it is almost entirely shaded out of existence except along rides, firebreaks, woodland margins and under the deciduous larches. Yet in the forest's very early stages the flora is truly happy: with the sheep excluded, probably for the first time in centuries, many plants can at last grow to their full height. The result is a great increase in berries, seeds and invertebrates, and hence in birds and mammals. Indeed for the birds it is more than a mere increase, it is the creation of a completely new population of woodlanders – robin, blackbird, song thrush, hedge sparrow, wren, various warblers and finches (especially lesser redpoll), tree pipit,

Pied flycatcher. Coming in April from Africa this is one of the Park's most characteristic birds. It uses nest boxes or natural holes in trees, especially in oakwoods. The male, seen here, is black and white, the female brown and white

blackcock and others, nesting once more in areas from which they were expelled by the clearance of the forests of long ago.

Sadly, this phase so rich in wildlife lasts a few years only. The little conifers soon bush into each other to form dark, dense, foodless thickets unacceptable to most birds. The next stage is when the trees grow tall and approach maturity, but the variety of birds remains very limited. There are many siskins, goldcrests and coal tits and a few crossbills; and on the edges of the forest a scattering of robins, chaffinches and others. Larger birds include magpie, carrion crow, jay, sparrowhawk and an occasional pair of buzzards. And one rarity, the goshawk, may have begun to breed in the older plantations. But even in spring and summer the vast interiors of the forests are depressingly lifeless and silent. Then after forty or fifty years the trees are felled block by block, the area is replanted and the cycle begins again.

In happy contrast with mature conifer plantations the old oakwoods of the valleysides are rich in birds, especially in spring and early summer when the leaves are being eaten by multitudes of nutritious caterpillars. There are various tits, finches and warblers, three kinds of woodpecker as well as nuthatch, tree creeper, jay, woodcock, tawny owl and other birds typical of southern Britain. But what gives these Welsh woods a touch of distinction is the presence here of numerous buzzards, pied flycatchers, redstarts and wood warblers. After the silence of the spruce woods it is a joy to hear all the songs and calls of the oakwood birds in spring. But even in the oakwoods one famous woodland bird is regrettably absent: Snowdonia is much too far north and west to come within the range of the nightingale.

The oakwoods belong to the lowland farming zone and many of the sylvan birds come out to forage daily in the fields along with more typical farmland birds like lapwings, curlews, pied wagtails and skylarks. Some visiting birdwatchers may note with surprise the absence or scarcity of common partridge, red-legged partridge, yellow wagtail, turtle dove, lesser whitethroat and tree sparrow. Even the house sparrow can be looked for in vain in much of the Park.

From autumn to spring it is the estuaries that are the Park's best birding spots and it is well to remember that in this context 'autumn' begins in mid-July with the return of the first passage waders from the north. Three estuaries are particularly rewarding: the Conwy in the north; the Dwyryd in the centre; and the Dyfi in the south. Three others, the Artro at Llanbedr, the Mawddach near Barmouth and the Broadwater near Tywyn, are certainly worth looking at but are not usually as rewarding as the others, probably because they are more sand than mud and therefore offer less food for birds. At Porthmadog what is left of the Glaslyn estuary occasionally turns up some good things.

Everywhere the peak months for passage species are August–September and April–May. The main winter bird gatherings last from November to February. The most numerous winter ducks are wigeon, mallard and teal. In summer you may see family parties of mallard, shelducks and red-breasted mergansers. The most abundant passage and winter waders are dunlin, redshank, curlew and oystercatcher. Smaller numbers of the less common ducks and waders are widely scattered and there is ever the hope of spotting a rarity among them. What few geese come to Snowdonia are usually on the Dyfi estuary, most of them whitefronts. Some estuaries have large roosts of gulls. The most frequent raptors are kestrel, sparrowhawk, peregrine, hen harrier and merlin; among the rare ones are osprey and marsh harrier.

Just outside the park along the shore from Bangor east to Llanfairfechan stretch the Lavan Sands (Traeth Lafan) where at low tide a huge extent of mud is uncovered – the feeding grounds from autumn to spring of a multitude of waders and other shore birds. The shallow returning tide brings with it large and varied gatherings of ducks and sometimes terns, gulls and notable numbers of great crested grebes and red-throated divers, making this by far the most bird-rich area of mudflats on the coast of north-west Wales.

The Park's only sea cliffs – they stretch for about seven miles from Friog south to Tonfannau – are insignificant and in places crumbling; and at low tide they look down on shingly beaches, not on water. As such they are unattractive to most seabirds and are nested on only by a scattering of fulmars and herring gulls. So to find a really impressive seabird colony we actually have to go inland 4 miles to Craig yr Aderyn (Bird Rock), a gaunt precipice above the flat valley of the Dysynni. Here cormorants – at present they number forty or so pairs – may have nested since prehistoric times when the sea washed the foot of these cliffs. Certainly the birds have been known here for three hundred years and are a splendid sight far overhead, gliding into the nests amid welcoming guttural cries. Or if you are energetic enough you can follow a footpath that puts you right on the summit and from up there you can look down on these admirable birds from high above. Up there too you get a whiff of one of nature's richest odours – the unique stench of a seabird colony. But this is a commune of one species only and to find really mixed groups of breeding seabirds you need to go right out of the Park to the majestic cliffs of the Great and Little Ormes at Llandudno; or Puffin Island off Anglesey; or Carreg y Llam along the north coast of

Lleyn, 15 miles south-west of Caernarfon; or Pen Cilan on Lleyn's southern side, 9 miles south-west of Pwllheli.

By a quirk of history the thought of seabirds might well take us back to where this chapter started, on the summit of Snowdon. A sight that would have astonished the tourists of the past and yet is so common-place to us today are the many gulls – herring, lesser black-backed and black-headed – which, mainly since World War II, have learnt to hang about tamely waiting for scraps at picnickers' parties all the way up the trails to the top of the mountain. It is a lifestyle that may well have its origins in the gulls' ancient habit of making daily flights to the hills after the breeding season. Up there they find caterpillars and beetles abundant in the grasslands; or they simply rest and moult many of their feathers.

Mammals

Until about 1700, red and roe deer roamed wild in Snowdonia; but these days the only deer are fallow, the descendants of those formerly kept in parks. Most numerous are those which originated in the deer-park at Nannau and are now living wild in the plantations of Coed y Brenin north of Dolgellau and east towards Llanuwchllyn. They have all the shyness of true wild deer and your best chance of spotting them is soon after dawn. After that they melt back into the shadows of the forest.

The only other large wild mammals are goats, but they too were introduced by man. Formerly they were kept on the hills in large numbers but fell out of favour at the end of the eighteenth century. Ever since then a few have been allowed to live perfectly wild because the traditional wisdom of shepherds is that goats, being more agile than sheep, crop the vegetation off dangerous ledges and so make such places less tempting to sheep, which are distinctly accident-prone on slippery rocks. The goats are a splendid sight to see when posed on rocky skylines, the long curved horns of the billies making them look just like ibexes in the Alps. They live in small herds (evidently of low fertility) and are best known on Glyder, Snowdon (the Beddgelert side), Rhinog and Rhobell Fawr. But although most remain faithful to their ancestral stamping grounds there is a strong gypsy streak in a few, especially the males, and so they are seen at times on other hills like Moelwyn, Cader Idris and, outside the Park, on Yr Eifl. Mostly wild and unapproachable in summer, they come down into the valleys in hard weather and often lose their shyness in their desperate search for food.

Nearly all the truly wild mammals are nocturnal and therefore difficult to observe. You may see foxes occasionally, for they do venture out by day, especially in quiet places. They are found from the coast to the mountains and, despite relentless persecution by farmers, keep up their numbers amazingly. Badgers, unknown on the uplands, are well established in ancient strongholds in some of the valley woodlands. The polecat, which these days is the special mammal of Wales because nearly exterminated in the rest of Britain, seems to be common throughout Snowdonia, probably outnumbering stoat and weasel. But their cousin, the pine marten, though formerly abundant, is now an extreme rarity of the wilder rocky places and woodlands. Another predator, the otter, though it has gone since mid-century from many of the English rivers, still thrives here at least locally.

Last century, mountain hares from Scotland and Ireland were liberated on Glyder and the Carneddau for sporting purposes but they have long ago died out. The native brown hare is widespread from the lowlands to the semi-uplands but nowhere seems common. Rabbits are mainly lowlanders: almost wiped out by myxomatosis in the 1950s they have now largely mastered this disease and are once again abundant.

You would be very lucky to see the native red squirrel anywhere in the Park today. Formerly common here it was gradually replaced by the American grey squirrel from mid-century onwards. The grey is especially abundant in broad-leaved woodlands but you could meet with wandering individuals even on the highest mountains because, perhaps under the stress of hunger, this thrustful rodent sometimes quits the trees for the open moors in search of new worlds to conquer. Alleged hybrids between red and grey squirrels, though frequently reported, are in fact young greys which show large areas of red in their pelage.

Offshore from Porthmadog to Aberdyfi you may sometimes see grey seals, but there are very few of them here because this part of the Cardigan Bay coast lacks the high cliffs, deep seas and breeding caves so loved by the many seals of Pembrokeshire and out west around Bardsey Island. Seals are not the only mammals in these waters but it is they alone that deliberately venture on to the land. The others are cetaceans – whales, dolphins and porpoises – and they come ashore only when stranded by the waves. The one most likely to be seen as it rolls up out of the water momentarily is the bottle-nosed dolphin, but half a dozen other cetaceans have occurred in Cardigan Bay.

Anyone looking for a rewarding mammals project might well consider a survey of one of the small rodents, insectivores or bats, for the detailed distribution of even the commonest is little known, especially

67

their altitudinal range. Particularly desirable is information about some of the rarer ones such as dormouse, yellow-necked mouse, harvest mouse, water shrew and lesser horseshoe bat. The bats are notoriously elusive and are unique in the habit some of them have of spending summer and winter in totally different habitats. The lesser horseshoe, for instance, often breeds in the roofs of houses but hibernates in old mines.

Reptiles and amphibians

The Park's four species of reptiles lead such inconspicuous lives it is not surprising that much remains to be discovered about the details of their distribution. The common lizard is probably the most numerous because it is found in a wide variety of open habitats, including both dry banks and sphagnum bogs, from coastal dunes, railway banks and roadsides up to well into the hill country. Its legless cousin, the slow worm, being nocturnal, is far less obvious though in some localities it may well outnumber the common lizard. It seems however to be restricted to the lowlands. There is no doubt that many slow worms get killed by people who mistake them for young adders.

The only two snakes found in Snowdonia – adder and grass snake – seem to be very local and generally scarce, though both are liable to have an occasional summer when they are much commoner than usual. The adder lives in a wide range of habitats – peat bogs, hedgerows, the banks of roads and railways, clearings in woods and on the lower moors. It is most likely to be seen when sunning itself in spring. Grass snakes enjoy being near water when they can hunt for frogs, their favourite food. But they will also live in open woodlands and hedgerows and often come into gardens to lay their eggs in the warmth of compost heaps.

The Park certainly has three widespread amphibians – common frog, common toad and palmate newt. Almost as certainly there are no crested newts at all, while the paucity of smooth newt records suggests it is either very local or rare. Some reports of it may have been erroneous, for palmate and smooth newts have often been confused. Frogs and palmate newts are found from the coast to the mountains: a frog was seen on Carnedd Llywelyn at 2,900ft (880m) and at nearly the same height palmate newts are reported from Aran Fawddwy. The toad, it seems, is a lowlander with no mountaineering ambitions whatever.

Fish

By far the most abundant freshwater fish in Snowdonia is the brown trout. It is much sought after by anglers and is found in nearly all streams and lakes except the few that are too acid for it. In the most fertile waters it reaches several pounds in weight but where the feeding is meagre the trout may never exceed a few ounces no matter how long it lives. Some rivers are famous for the sea trout (or sewin) which is generally regarded as a migratory form of the brown trout. By feeding in the rich waters of the ocean these sea trout attain up to three times the size of brown trout and are fished for in the estuaries by seine netting, a method virtually unchanged perhaps since prehistoric days. The fish that get past the nets then go upriver to face all the perils of rod and line angling. The best sea trout river in north Wales is acknowledged to be the Dyfi.

Also caught in the seine nets are the salmon, which can grow to 40lb (18kg) or more. They too are ocean-going fish which need to come into fresh water to spawn and, like the sea trout, often penetrate far upstream, negotiating cascades and the lesser waterfalls right to high moorlands where the tributaries are so shallow that the salmons' backs stick out of the water. In such vulnerable situations many of them used to be gaffed out by the upland people in the days when the hills were more populated than they are today. The fish were mostly taken in late autumn and then smoked to keep them for eating in winter. In recent years the number of salmon coming into the rivers from the sea has declined because their long-unknown ocean feeding grounds have been discovered and the fish are being taken commercially on a big scale. With fewer salmon occupying the spawning places – the gravelly beds of streams – there is now more room for the sea trout which seem to have increased accordingly.

Two other members of the salmon family are rare. One has a Welsh name only, *gwyniad*, which might be translated as 'whiting', a reference to its silvery appearance. It grows to about a foot in length and is found only in the lake at Bala where it lives in shoals in the depths. It feeds on minute forms of life and scorns all the lures of anglers. It used to be caught wholesale in nets for local hotels but it is not the most tasty of fish and has long been out of fashion. The other very local fish is the char: it too is a gregarious species of deep lakes, coming into the shallows only for breeding in early winter. It is native only in Llyn Cwellyn (between Caernarfon and Beddgelert) and Llyn Padarn, Llanberis. Before the coming of the hydro-electric project at Dinorwig there were also

69

The gwyniad, a member of the salmon family, is found in Wales only in Bala Lake where, though abundant, it is little known because it is not attracted by the lures of anglers

char in Llyn Peris. But because this scheme made the lake unsuitable for them the char were transferred in 1978 (via a hatchery) to Ffynnon Llugwy, a corrie lake 6 miles away on the Carneddau.

Two American members of the salmon family, the rainbow trout and the brook trout, have been put into some lakes to improve the fishing. Another salmonid introduction is the grayling. Though a widespread native in Britain it is not indigenous in Snowdonia. It was put into the lake at Bala last century and there it still thrives, though usually grayling live in quite swift rivers.

What are poorly represented in Snowdonia are the many coarse fish so typical of lowland England. Only in Bala Lake, by far the Park's richest water, are there plenty of coarse fish. In this deep, 4-mile-long water, besides members of the salmon family, there are perch, roach, pike, gudgeon, eels, lampreys, stone loaches, minnows and bullheads. Even rudd and silver bream have recently been introduced. And in Trawsfynydd reservoir there are perch and grass carp. But elsewhere in the Park coarse fish are very sparse. Locally there are minnows (even in some mountain lakes), stone loaches and three-spined sticklebacks. The ten-spined stickleback is found in brackish ditches by estuaries. And in the estuaries themselves are typically bass, flounders, grey mullet, sea lamprey, garfish, smelt and eels. The seas off north Wales are rich in fish and angling is very popular.

Butterflies and moths

A fine selection of butterflies may be seen in and around Snowdonia. This is especially true if we go a little outside the Park to include the limestone region of the Great Orme with its strong colonies of the brown argus and of small races of the grayling and the silver-studded blue. The common blue may be seen throughout lowland Snowdonia but is especially abundant in the coastal dunes. The holly blue is widespread but nowhere seems to be common. In many of the oakwoods there are plenty of purple hairstreaks but you really need binoculars to see them as they flutter tantalisingly above the tree tops in July. Much more local is the green hairstreak: it flies in a variety of open, sunny

The scarlet tiger is a startling moth when the sun catches its bright-red underwings as it flies in the June sunlight. It is found mainly in damp habitats where its caterpillar feeds on comfrey, nettles and other plants

In late spring and early summer the wood tiger moth flies both by day and night on moorlands and in open woods. The caterpillar, a blackish 'woolly-bear', feeds on a wide variety of plants in late summer and again in early spring

This female emperor moth, mainly pale-grey and white, has just emerged from her cocoon. The scent she emits will attract males (smaller but more colourful) as they fly over the heather moors in the sunlight of early spring

habitats, even up to fairly high moorlands. But only the small heath is widespread and common on the uplands. Any whites you see up there are likely to be migrants and in some years you may find small tortoise-shells abundant at the heather flowers in August. The peacock is numerous in the lowlands and in far smaller numbers there are the comma and the dark-green and silver-washed fritillaries.

Local bogs have marsh and small pearl-bordered fritillaries and, especially rare, the large heath. The fields have orange tips, meadow browns, hedge browns (or gatekeepers), small coppers and large skippers. Lanesides are a favourite haunt of wall browns and ringlets; dry slopes, especially by the sea, have graylings; and in all broad-leaved woods you should find the green-veined white and the speckled wood. The brimstone is generally scarce, its best locality probably being the Ganllwyd valley north of Dolgellau. Most summers bring at least a few migrant red admirals and painted ladies but the clouded yellow gets to Snowdonia only in very exceptional years.

The Park's moths are multitudinous and there is space here to mention only a few of the upland species which, as adults or caterpillars, might be spotted by hill walkers. Conspicuous, especially in the large, hairy larval stage, are fox, drinker and northern eggar, for they feed boldly in broad daylight with never a thought of concealment. In the adult stage the northern eggar flies wildly about in the July sunshine and might easily be mistaken for a butterfly. Another large daylight flyer, but of early spring, is the male emperor which dashes about over the heather trying to scent out a female. In summer its brilliant green caterpillars, spotted red or yellow, feed openly on heather, bilberry and other plants. Among the smaller moths of the hills are: ruby tiger, wood tiger, clouded buff, flounced rustic, July highflyer, northern spinach, true-lovers' knot, antler, Haworth's minor, common heath and many others. Ashworth's rustic is a Snowdonia speciality.

4
SNOWDONIA'S NATURE RESERVES

If you come from some far-off city, Snowdonia may seem a quiet Shangri-La where life goes on with little change. But then perhaps you arrive at Trawsfynydd and there, amid wild moorlands and mountains, what do you find but a huge and ugly nuclear power-station. So you learn that despite its status as a National Park Snowdonia enjoys no immunity from the devastations of science and technology. It is the same with all its wildlife habitats – heather moors, plant-rich crags, oakwoods, herb-rich meadows, peat bogs, sand dunes and estuaries – they have to be battled for incessantly.

This chapter gives a brief account of the national nature reserves of the Nature Conservancy Council (NCC). Several of them, especially the mountain reserves, can be visited without a permit. But for most of the others a permit is required if you wish to stray from the public paths which cross them. Two other organisations, the North Wales Naturalists' Trust and the Royal Society for the Protection of Birds, also have reserves in and near the Park. And there is one Country Park: it is across the lake from Llanberis and includes an attractive stretch of steep old woodland near an abandoned slate quarry. For addresses to write to about visiting the Park's reserves see Appendix 2.

Cwm Idwal (SH 6459)

No permit is required. Scenic splendours unfold one after another as you travel along A5 from Capel Curig to Bethesda. For 7 miles the

north-eastern flank of the Glyder range is scooped out by a succession
of majestic corries with the showpiece of them all in the centre, as you
find when you get round the skirts of Tryfan and see the crags above
Cwm Idwal coming into view. This famous mountain hollow, whose
floor is 1,200ft (365m) above sea level, is reached by a footpath which
in half a mile lifts you gently from near the youth hostel on A5 to the
shores of Llyn Idwal. A booklet obtainable from the Nature Conservancy Council describes what you can see along the nature trail that
curves round this crag-shadowed lake. Cwm Idwal was the first national
nature reserve in Wales (declared 1954) and is certainly one of the
finest. It belongs to the National Trust and is leased to the NCC.

As you circle the lake you are very much on the trail of the Great Ice
Age. Everywhere you see moraines, screes, scratched rocks, erratic
boulders and *roches moutonnées*. The glaciers could have melted only
yesterday, so clear is the evidence of their work. And from all along the
trail you look up at the vertical chasm called Twll Du (the Devil's
Kitchen) and see how the rock layers on either side of it form a symmetrical downfold or syncline suggesting the former existence of some high
mountain range now almost completely destroyed by the ravages of 300
million years.

For centuries Cwm Idwal has been grazed by sheep (and formerly
many goats of which only a handful now remain) and all this nibbling
has had a depressing effect on the vegetation. To illustrate this the
NCC has set up small fenced enclosures and now you can contrast the
short turf outside the fence with the jungle of tall grass, heather and
other plants inside. In time perhaps rowans and birches will colonise
these enclosures – a reminder of the woodland which probably once
covered much of this corrie.

Long before anyone studied its rocks or its Ice Age effects, Cwm
Idwal was known among botanists for the luxuriance and variety of the
flora of the Devil's Kitchen, though they usually called these cliffs
Trigyfylchau ('the three clefts'). The damp ledges of these crags of
volcanic rock (the Bedded Pyroclastic Series) are as crowded with
mountain plants as anywhere in Wales. Common among them are the
starry and mossy saxifrages, roseroot, mountain sorrel, alpine meadow-
rue and northern bedstraw; others such as the arctic saxifrage and the
Snowdon lily are much harder to find.

As you follow the trail anticlockwise past the Devil's Kitchen you see
a change in the cliffs. Now instead of shattered precipices and screes
you come to a sweep of harder, smoother rocks that reach far up the
slopes of Glyder Fawr. They are solidified acidic lavas of a type called

Cwm Idwal national nature reserve is a corrie showing many features of glaciation such as the lake and the heaped-up moraines beyond. The downfolded volcanic rocks of the Devil's Kitchen cliffs, evidence of the Snowdon syncline, are well-known for their arctic-alpine plants

rhyolite (Tryfan is of the same rock) and because they offer good hand-holds and toe-holds, and are not terrifyingly steep, these Idwal Slabs have long been popular as a nursery for novice climbers. Hard, dry and limeless, the Slabs are just the sort of rocks that most alpine plants detest and you will find little else there but sparse heather, bilberry and wavy hair-grass.

Llyn Idwal, though rather shallow, is a fine example of a corrie lake with pure and fertile water. On its boggy margins you will find such plants as marsh cinquefoil, bogbean, various sedges and two insect-eaters: common butterwort and round-leaved sundew. In or near the water grow quillwort, shoreweed, lobelia, floating water-plantain, awlwort and a minute unfernlike fern called pillwort. In the clear shallows you can see shoals of lively minnows – not a common fish in most of Snowdonia's lakes – and there are trout in the deeper water. Cormorants and herons drop in for a meal at times. Common sand-pipers breed along the lake edge in spring. Winter brings a few ducks and whooper swans if the lake is not frozen. The cliffs above the lake are nesting places for raven and ring ouzel. Wheatears are numerous in the screes. Choughs are frequent summer visitors, foraging on the grasslands round the lake.

Snowdon (SH 6054)

No permit is required. Snowdon's unique starfish pattern of high ridges separated by huge hollows makes for great scenery and offers many a challenge to walkers and climbers. But there is much more to it than that. Geologists, for instance, see Snowdon as a major exposure of very varied rocks whose problems and complexities are infinite. For ecologists much of the mountain's fascination arises from the distinction between the vegetation of its limeless rocks (slates, rhyolites and granites) and that of the lime-yielding rocks (the Bedded Pyroclastic Series and some of the dolerites and basalts). For botanists the most intriguing aspect of Snowdon is that although so southern and so near the Atlantic it still remains, ten thousand years after the Ice Age, an acceptable refuge for alpine plants though the climate is on the whole quite unalpine, its summers too cool and wet, its winters not reliably cold and snowy. Clearly Snowdon's alpines are a very adaptable group whose survival raises interesting questions. And also on the high ledges there are the many plants which, far from being alpines, are really lowlanders with ambitions to scale the heights. How long have they been mountaineering and are they destined to replace all the alpines some day?

Like those elsewhere in the Park, the plant-rich crags of Snowdon mostly face east or north-east: Clogwyn Du'r Arddu; the east face of Snowdon itself (Clogwyn y Garnedd); part of the cliffs of Lliwedd; and the corries along the south-west side of Llanberis Pass. As these are the sites that were visited by the very earliest mountain botanists it is good to think that they are now safeguarded as a part of this finest of all the reserves.

Cwm Glas Crafnant (SH 7360)

A permit is required for the enclosed woodland. Llyn Crafnant is hemmed in narrowly by steep slopes. But above the head of the lake a splendid corrie opens out with a rough and knobbly skyline of grey rocks and cliffs with vast tumbles of pallid stones below them as well as huge block scree full of dark and cavernous depths. Below the scree the slopes are bouldery and covered largely by oak; but there are also patches of pure ashwood, a sign of the liminess of the soil of these

Llyn Crafnant, three miles south-west of Trefri in the Conwy valley, is one of Snowdonia's loveliest waters and the starting point for several first-class walks. On the far hillside is Cwm Glas Crafnant national nature reserve

volcanic rocks, as on parts of Creigiau Gleision, a mile to the north.

Dog's-mercury, sanicle and other calcicoles grow among the trees and, uniquely in upland Snowdonia, you will see (June to August) masses of the showy, purple-veined, white flowers of the wood vetch. Look amongst the cool, damp fissures in the cliffs for stone bramble, green spleenwort and hard shield-fern. Wet flushes in pastures below the woods have countless heath spotted and a few fragrant orchids. The small white orchid has been found here and so has the frog orchid but both are extremely elusive. As summer turns towards autumn these wet slopes are beautiful with the solitary white flowers of the grass of Parnassus which, outside Anglesey, is a really rare plant in Wales.

Rhinog (SH 6530)

No permit is required. Not only the area included in the national nature reserve but the whole district around is worth seeing if you enjoy high, heathy moorlands. For up here on Rhinog, despite some local losses, much heather flourishes still, a waist-deep jungle of leggy stems which eventually die of old age but are replaced by copious regeneration. The heather's survival here is no mystery. This is an upland whose poverty is unequalled anywhere in Wales over such a large extent – great unfarmable and unforestable spreads of quite naked rock, or rock concealed by the thinnest of thin soils. And there are crags, screes, perched boulders and many other signs of the ice-sheets which denuded the landscape instead of plastering it with clay. Riding up the nearby coast in the twelfth century Giraldus Cambrensis, when he reached Llanfair, summed up the Rhinog perfectly when he declared it to be 'the roughest and harshest district in all Wales'.

Botanists revere this wild northern half of Rhinog for its many varied mosses and lichens which live deep in half-hidden fissures or in the shelter of heather. And also under the heather you may find the lesser twayblade, one of the scarcer orchids of Wales. The many rock-girt lakes and lakelets of these uplands, though at first sight rather plantless, are worth exploring for quillworts, shoreweed, lobelia, pondweeds and floating water-plantain. The bogs have sundews, sedges and many other treasures. Fern rarities include royal fern and, unusually high, the Tunbridge filmy-fern.

A characteristic bird is the ring ouzel (listen for his insistently repeated note); and you will probably meet with a few red grouse, though they are nothing like as abundant as in the game-preserving days of early this century. There are also ravens and buzzards, and with luck you might see a merlin. A herd of shaggy, multicoloured, feral goats has long roamed these untamed hills.

Cader (Cadair) ldris (SH 7213)

A permit is required for the enclosed woodland. It is along the magnificent Cader range that Snowdonia's igneous rocks come to their southern limit. From Dolgellau you see them at their scenic best, a line of naked precipices of a hard, crystalline, granite-like rock called granophyre which is not common elsewhere in the Park. For a close look at this rock make your way up to Llyn y Gadair, a corrie lake with good crags horse-shoed around it. This granophyre (with dolerite) escarpment is only a part of Cader's igneous make-up. There are also the lavas, both acid and basic, which flowed out of Cader's now lost volcano, and the ashes that exploded from it. And there are sedimentary rocks, chiefly mudstones, sandwiched amongst the others. Metamorphic rocks in the form of slate can be seen exposed in the disused quarry above Arthog.

Like the Park's other igneous mountains, Cader is a hugger-mugger of mainly limeless rocks and a few that yield enough lime to make life possible for plants such as green spleenwort, brittle bladder-fern, mountain sorrel, mossy saxifrage, lesser meadow-rue and purple saxifrage. All these are local but not nearly as restricted as three other calcicoles – moss campion, alpine meadow-rue and alpine saw-wort – which are truly rare here. Two distinguished calcifuges of Cader's peak are dwarf willow (very hard to find) and, much easier, the stiff sedge (which is not nearly stiff enough to defy the ever-nibbling sheep).

If you scramble to the top of Cader from the Dolgellau side up that toilsome scree, the Foxes' Path, you find that the summit ridge is well on its way to becoming a knife-edge like Lliwedd or Crib Goch. You see too that the south side is even more spectacular than the north. Here is Cwm Cau whose cliffs curve round a majestic corrie with a deep, cold lake in its hollow. From the lake a stream goes splashing down the cwm and then, because this is a hanging valley, it reaches a lip and suddenly throws itself down falls and cascades all the way to the bottom of Talyllyn Pass, much of its course shadowed by broad-leaved, mossy woodland. Blessed by such drama in its scenery and such variety in its ecology, Cader is a first-class mountain from top to bottom.

Coed Ganllwyd (SH 7224)

No permit is required. A part of the National Trust's Dolmelynllyn estate, 5 miles north of Dolgellau, this rocky oakwood, green-floored with moss and ferns, is reached up a steep winding lane which leaves A470 at the south end of Ganllwyd village (car park on the main road). The stream, torrenting down the slopes of Y Llethr, is the Gamlan which comes roaring over high ledges of black rock to make the double fall called Rhaeadr Ddu, which has attracted sightseers for two hundred years. Here came the fern-collectors also and since then the bryologists have recorded a wealth of mosses and liverworts.

Coed Cymerau (SH 6842)

A permit is required away from the public footpath. This wood lies a mile north-west of Ffestiniog and has much in common with Coed Ganllwyd – lots of rain, an acid soil, shadowing oaks, bare grey rocks, a spray-damp gorge, a thunderous stream and carpets of mosses and ferns. Bilberry sprawls down one side of the gorge, purple moorgrass down the other. A footbridge at the bottom sets you on the path up through the trees to Dduallt station, site of the famous spiral on the Ffestiniog railway. Coed Cymerau has long been popular and there is a car park at Rhyd-y-sarn on A496.

Coed Camlyn (SH 6539)

A permit is required. Though Coed Camlyn, half a mile south-west of Maentwrog, has neither torrent nor gorge, its steep slopes, scattered with cliffy outcrops half-hidden among the trees, are cool and damp. Bilberry and brambles cover much of the ground and oak, birch, rowan, hazel and holly are happily regenerating. As in so many of Snowdonia's woodlands, the trees are spindly and multi-trunked and were probably cut and cut again for the oakbark trade of past centuries.

When you have looked at Coed Camlyn it is well worth while to make the further effort of getting up through the bracken and heather to the top of Pen-y-foel, which has an unrivalled view north to the crags of Moelwyn and south to the ramparts of Rhinog, deeply hollowed by the great corrie of Cwm Moch.

Coedydd Maentwrog (SH 6641)

No permit is required. Tourists of the Romantic period adored fertile valleys whose slopes were bosomy with broad-leaved woods: hence their passion for the Vale of Ffestiniog, which mercifully is still very leafy. Not that there is any miracle about the survival of these miles of woods. Early on it was due to the care of the owners of the Tan-y-bwlch estate and recently it is thanks to conservation bodies such as the National Trust, the Nature Conservancy Council and the North Wales Naturalists' Trust.

These woods can be compared and contrasted with Coed Camlyn on the opposite side of the vale. South-facing and with evidently deeper and drier soil, the warm Coedydd Maentwrog woodlands are floored by bracken rather than bilberry. Otherwise they resemble Camlyn in being a haven for foxes, badgers and polecats and in having their leaves chewed in spring by battalions of caterpillars that are the food of many songbirds. Footpaths contour through the trees starting either from near the Oakeley Arms or the woodland lake called Llyn Mair, or from Tan-y-bwlch station on the narrow gauge railway. These paths go on beyond the reserve nearly up to Blaenau Ffestiniog, keeping under trees all the way.

Coed y Rhygen (SH 6737)

A permit is required. This wood on the west side of Trawsfynydd reservoir is reached by the lane round the reservoir from Trawsfynydd or by the footpath past the power-station. A rugged wilderness of hard, limeless Cambrian grits forms the northern end of Rhinog. Everywhere you encounter wide sheets of grey rock where nothing at all grows except those strangest and most enduring of all plants – the encrusting lichens. But where these inhospitable rocks come down to the lake they have folded into ridges and troughs in whose hollows enough soil and humus have gathered to allow the development of a sessile oakwood which looks as if it may have been there since prehistory, so primeval is its atmosphere. Not that its individual trees are all that old for they may well have been felled repeatedly. But their roots are probably ancient beyond the telling.

For a north Wales oakwood, Coed y Rhygen stands high and its stunted trees bend away from more wind, rain and snow than any of the other woodland reserves have to endure. So its fascination is that of a wood struggling to survive against extremes of poverty and climate. Inevitably here is mainly a world of non-flowering plants. Ferns abound, including filmy-ferns; and forests of polypodies wave to you from most of the trees. The boulders and tree trunks deeply upholstered with mosses remind us of another primitive grove – Wistman's Wood high on Dartmoor.

Coed Dolgarrog (SH 7666)

A permit is required away from public paths. The slopes of Foel Grach on the Carneddau drop steeply east to a moorland shelf whose forests were probably shaved off very early, for there is a long history of human settlement up there. But where this plateau suddenly drops into the Conwy valley you find the whole escarpment deeply clothed by the trees of Coed Dolgarrog, a wood whose flora includes a wider range of species than is usual in Snowdonia's woodlands. There are patches of soft shield-fern, ramsons, woodruff, strawberry and sanicle, all pointers to the soil being a little sweeter than in most areas of the Park. The geology map shows why. For although the wood is partly on acid lavas, there is a central craggy area of basic volcanic rock where the soils are blessed with enough calcium to discourage the all-smothering bilberry and give heart to a few of the lime-seekers. The trees too are more than usually varied. Both pedunculate and sessile oaks are present and there is much beech, elm and sycamore – tall elegant specimens that are still aspiring upwards.

The southern edge of Coed Dolgarrog extends an arm towards the moorlands and is quite different from the rest of the wood. As you make your way up the valley of the Afon Ddu you soon wish you had come in your wellies when you say goodbye to the oaks and find yourself floundering amongst swamps and alders. Such woods used to be much commoner when they were preserved for the clog-making trade but now nobody wants them, which is sad because they are fascinating places with their own special wildlife: they attract siskins in winter and they have orchids, marsh hawk's-beard and other flowers to make colour under the summer trees.

Coed Gorswen (SH 7570)

A permit is required away from the public path. Coed Gorswen lies 5 miles south of Conwy. Hart's-tongue fern, black bryony, shining crane's-bill, woodruff and lords and ladies greet you up the leafy lane to Gorswen farm which is your access route if you are a permit holder. They are a sign that the soil here, by Snowdonian standards, is truly fertile. Sure enough when you get into this damp-floored wood you find a profusion of these plants along with much dog's-mercury, sanicle, wood melick and primrose – a striking contrast with the smothering mosses or bilberry of acid-soiled woods. Coed Gorswen likewise escapes the dominance of the sessile oak: there is much pedunculate oak along with wych elm, ash and hazel. The soil hereabouts has come down as glacial drift from areas of basic volcanic rock on the slopes of the Carneddau. And from those slopes you can look down on Coed Gorswen and see how it slopes gently towards the Conwy across the wide and verdant basin around the village of Ro-wen.

Coedydd Aber (SH 6671)

No permit is required for this reserve 6 miles east of Bangor. 'I saw it in its highest perfection in the wet season of August 1799, when the violent torrent washed down three bridges between the falls and the sea. One of the bridges was that on the great post road to Ireland.' So wrote William Hutton on one of his visits to Snowdonia from Birmingham. Since then thousands have enjoyed this oakwood glen that climbs towards the Carneddau and is lively with cascades and cataracts all the way to the great fall. Here the stream drops over a sill of the igneous rock called granophyre which has endured while sedimentary rocks upstream and down have been washed away long ago.

The soils of Coedydd Aber are mainly acid but there are enough slightly limy patches to ensure quite a varied flora. But the glen is best known for its western-type mosses and liverworts which rejoice in the spray of the falls. A nature trail (informative leaflet available) leads from the car park up to the waterfall which drops down the cliffs of Creigiau Rhaeadr Fawr. Above the falls is treeless moorland (with pre-historic settlements) rising to Foel Grach and Foel Fras.

Coed Tremadog (SH 5640)

A permit is required. A long rampart of handsome, south-facing cliffs with their feet almost at sea level stands behind the village of Tre-madog, 1 mile north of Porthmadog. The upper half of these crags rise high as clean rock faces but their lower parts are hidden under a chaotic tumble of scree that varies in size from quite small stones to chunks the size of cottages. It all looks unpromising ground for anything except a few mosses and lichens yet somehow much of this rough scree has been colonised by thick woodland which in places has even scaled half-way up the cliffs.

The bulk of the rock here is igneous – a dolerite which is evidently somewhat limy as you realise when you see the generous clumps of rock stonecrop, shining crane's-bill, marjoram, orpine, soft shield-fern and hart's-tongue. Delightful too are the multitudinous ox-eye daisies that spread white curtains along the base of the crags. But you do not really need to enter this reserve to guess at the fertility of its soils: from the road alongside you see that here is one of the Park's rare ashwoods with a typical ground flora that includes dog's mercury and water avens. And among the ash trees there is much hazel, wild privet, spindle, wych elm, beech and sycamore. Elsewhere in the reserve, where the soils are more sour, the oak is dominant. Coed Tremadog's rocky wilderness is an ancient refuge for fox, badger and, on local hearsay, the ultra-rare pine marten. Some of the cliffs are huge vertical faces whose fissures are nightly roosts for ravens, choughs and a noisy throng of jackdaws. By day it is human climbers who swarm on the crags.

Downstream from Beddgelert the Pass of Aberglaslyn has been a tourists' Mecca for over two hundred years

Morfa Harlech (SH 5632)

A permit is required for part of this reserve, which is found a mile north-west of Harlech. From Harlech beach northwards at low tide there is a wonderful stretch of firm brown sands backed by dunes tightly bound most of the way by marram grass. It makes a superb walk on a fine clear day when ahead of you the distant houses of Cricieth are shining white in the sun and all the hills of Lleyn rise clear before you. But if you want to grasp the essence of this *morfa*, this 'sea-place', you should go on some less comfortable day when a south-west gale is doing its best to blind you with sand. For this is the wind which has built these unlive-able dunes and when it is actually at work you see how the dunes begin to take shape right out here on the open beach, though at first they reach no higher than a few inches around the dead seaweed and flotsam of the tideline.

A few yards inland the sand is piled round plants of lilac-flowered sea rocket and prickly saltwort. Behind that line the embryo dunes slope through a zone of long, lax couch-grass to where the forest of grey-green, wind-tossed marram grass begins. Here the sand is white, dry and loose under your feet and once you are over this first low dune barrier you find a different world. The sight, the noise and the smell of the sea have gone and now, as well as marram, you begin to see hound's-tongue, evening primrose, burnet rose, carline thistle, centaury, spurges and other delights of dunelands. And you exchange seashells for landshells, many of them prettily banded. Everywhere you go there are rabbit-holes and scuttling rabbits whose dominion in this sandy empire may date back centuries.

Over the next line of dunes is a different world again. Now instead of loose sand you find a tightly-knitted turf of grasses, lichens, mosses and other plants scattered with countless rabbit droppings – a remark-able stretch of vegetation that has learnt to live with very intensive grazing: hawk's-bit, lady's-bedstraw, stork's-bill, thyme, restharrow and many others that make these fixed dunes uniquely aromatic. Then at its heart this duneland falls away into a damp, lime-rich lowland full of creeping willow and tall, cruel clumps of sharp rush. Here in summer

The beautiful Cregennen Lakes near Arthog belong to the National Trust. The ridge beyond is Tyrau Mawr, part of the Cader Idris range

The rare Snowdon lily, an arctic-alpine found in Britain only in Snowdonia, flowers mainly in early June are countless orchids and dense patches of the lovely marsh helleborine. Autumn too has its delights: the blue of the devil's-bit scabious, the endearing little purple gentian called felwort and the shining black hips of the burnet rose. The survival of the rich flora of these dunes is enormously cheering when you think what botanical deserts nearly all the local farmlands have become in recent decades.

Inevitably with all this variety of dune flora there is a wealth of insects including many moths, butterflies and dragonflies. And, unusually in dunes, there is quite a varied population of breeding birds, mainly centred round one small lake where gulls and waders breed in spring amid the yellow flags, and ducks and a few whooper swans gather in winter.

Morfa Dyffryn (SH 5525)

A permit is required away from public footpaths. Much of what can be said of Morfa Harlech applies equally to Morfa Dyffryn, 5 miles south-west of Harlech. At Dyffryn, as at Harlech, the Atlantic gales have deposited a Sahara of sand just behind the shore. On the seaward side there is a line of tall, volatile dunes that are very vulnerable to human disturbance because their protective mantle of marram grass, though remarkably able to survive frequent burial in sand, cannot tolerate trampling.

As at Harlech there is a parallel range of dunes inland and between the two ridges stretch wide, damp hollows, lime-rich from powdered seashells and firmly turfed over with a very varied flora that is patchily dominated, though not suppressed, by carpets of creeping willow. Alongside all the commoners on this morfa, the more notable plants include variegated horsetail, sea holly, round-leaved wintergreen, felwort, angular Solomon's-seal, yellow bartsia, smooth cat's-ear and a grass called dune fescue. Amongst the orchids are marsh helleborine, green-flowered (or pendulous) helleborine, autumn lady's-tresses, pyramidal orchid and various marsh and spotted orchids. There are many moths, butterflies and other invertebrates.

Dyfi estuary (SN 6395)

This reserve stretches from Aberdyfi to Glandyfi. The Park begins and ends with beautiful estuaries. In the north is the Conwy, in the south the Dyfi. Both have wide spreads of saltmarsh plants; both have sands and muds lively with small creatures which have fascinating lifestyles and which are the food of many ducks, gulls and waders. What the Dyfi has in addition (just outside the Park boundary) are the plant-rich dunes of Ynys-las and, behind the seaside village of Borth, the miry wilderness of Cors Fochno. The Dyfi's special birds are the Greenland white-fronted geese which are here from mid-October to mid-April, this being their only regular Welsh wintering place. But they and the other estuary birds are not easy to observe, especially at low tide when they are out in the centre of the estuary. At high spring tides very good birdwatching is often possible from the south bank at the RSPB reserve at Ynys-hir (SN 6896) or at the estuary mouth at Ynys-las (SN 6094).

Among the dunes at Ynys-las there is an excellent visitor centre providing literature and information about the reserve's wildlife and conservation. You will need a permit to visit the peatlands of Cors Fochno whose main interests for most visitors are its flora and ecology. It is a paradise for plants which love to grow with their roots in ground as sour as vinegar: heather, sphagnum moss, bog rosemary, sundew, bladderwort, bogbean, sweet gale and a few sedges and orchids. Among the butterflies are the marsh fritillary and the large heath; and dragonflies are many. This fine bog, an amazing survival from prehistory, holds in its peat a vast store of information about past vegetation, climate and land use in the form of the pollen of many centuries of flowering plants and trees preserved in its airless depths. Its surface is a thin skin of plant life stretched over a quag that is 30ft (10m) deep at the centre. It has the slightly domed profile typical of unspoilt raised bogs and is the largest such area now left in Britain.

5

MONUMENTS OF FORMER DAYS

Tombs of a most ancient kind; standing stones of unknown meaning; mysterious cairns and circles; ancient trackways whose goal and purpose are conjectural; clusters of hut remains near the faint outlines of farmlands that had just emerged from the primal forest; the earliest of the hill-top strongholds; Roman camps and forts and the often dubious roads that linked them; the later native forts, still in use after Roman times; the first stones inscribed by Christians and sites of the Celtic churches; all the shattered walls, settlements and faint boundary dykes of the Dark Ages which were not too dark to produce the flowering of the Middle Ages in due course; the steadily evolving medieval landscape and cultivations; the first castle mounds still standing proud though their wooden towers rotted eight centuries ago; the great stone castles, Welsh and English, and the setting up of the boroughs; the medieval churches, at first so simple, then so ornate; the coming of villages and farmhouses not all that dissimilar from those we know today; the shaping of the present landscape with field walls snaking away over far horizons; the slow evolution of the roads; then the fine self-confidence of the bridge-builders who took the roads over the rivers and brought them right into our own time.

The field is rich indeed and wherever you go in Snowdonia you will find the palpable traces of those who have lived, worked, played, struggled, prospered or failed through all of five thousand years. And as you study the scene more closely and begin to get your eye in for detecting more subtle traces of the past, it may well be that you will discover things which no one has noticed before. For it is certain that there is still much that has not yet been revealed.

Megalithic tombs

Prominent among the relics of remote antiquity are the neolithic or New Stone Age tombs made up of three or four large upright stones with a sometimes colossal flat one placed neatly on top. So they have stood for maybe five thousand years; and if you enjoy thinking about time and eternity and the long flow of human generations, there is nothing more moving than these simple, enduring structures. Originally they were mounded over with earth or stones which have long since been dislodged or entirely removed. These tombs were never numerous in the Park. Doubtless some have been destroyed without trace. A few have slipped their capstones or lost them entirely, but even they have their deep appeal.

In the north there is Maen-y-bardd (SH 740718), a smallish but

One of the Park's few surviving dolmens, Maen-y-bardd is high above the Conwy valley near the ancient road through the pass of Bwlch y Ddeufaen

well-preserved cromlech, as these megaliths are called in Welsh. It looks down to the Conwy estuary from an open hillside high above Ro-wen. (When it was built, was this cromlech deep in the green-wood?) It stands, like so many antiquities, at the side of a prehistoric road. Close by and aligned upon it are two standing stones, but they could be a contribution of a thousand years later when the Bronze Age had arrived. For a more famous dolmen, because so much bigger and more complex, you must cross the wide Conwy valley and find your way up to Capel Garmon (SH 8154), 2 miles south-east of Betws-y-coed. This fine chambered tomb, in State care, has been well investigated and yielded valuable information. Like Maen-y-bardd it is high-placed and is worth visiting for its mountain views alone.

Over in the west, on the slopes between the Rhinog range and the coast, are several more megalithic tombs in various states of preservation. Easily the most accessible of them are the twin cromlechs just behind the school at Dyffryn (SH 588228). But if you have time it is worth the effort to seek out the two long cairns which lie side by side high on the moorland at Carneddau Hengwm (SH 613205). In their heyday they must have been huge, these piles of rocks heaped above a series of chambered tombs. Even today, with most of the stones pillaged to build nearby field walls, they are amongst the greatest cairns in Wales.

The Bronze Age

For those who feel the lure of ancient trackways there are two very rewarding ones to be explored in this south-west quarter of the Park. Both take you east over the hills from the coast: one creeping with difficulty round the north end of the Rhinogydd; the other, about six-teen miles south, slipping more easily round the north side of Cader Idris. To make sure you don't get lost the Bronze Age builders thought-fully provided standing stones and round cairns to mark your onward way; or, more likely, the stones and cairns were memorials set along the way where travellers would see and revere them, like the stones piled so conspicuously on many mountain tops. The more northerly of the roads is conjectured to have begun down at Mochras, a safe haven which may also have been used long before the Bronze Age by the ships of the megalith builders. The estuary at Mochras, now silted up, could well have been a port for the busy Bronze Age trade between Britain and Ireland.

The standing stones begin with a tall monolith in the field behind the filling station in Llanbedr (SH 583270), its smaller partner being rather doubtfully ancient. From here the surmised route went north-north-east, as indicated by two more stones, the second of which stands close to the mountain road that links Llanfair with Eisingrug. This stone is named on the map as Carreg (SH 598309), and in a few hundred yards you come to a very fine stone on the other side of the lane at the foot of Moel y Sensigl. Then there are five squat boulders leading you to the foot of Moel Goedog where you must leave the tarmac and follow the track north round the hill, encouraged by the sight of a stone circle (though much impoverished) on the left of the path.

For miles the track is a delicious green road over the moors towards a prominent hill called Moel y Geifr. And if you look back you see that Moel Goedog not only has the Bronze Age at its foot but also the Iron Age on its summit in the shape of the double banks of a hill fort. Your green road now rounds a shoulder and seems to be going straight for the crags of Moel Ysgyfarnogod ('the hill of the hares'), a curious name, for those high stony wastes look anything but hare country. Nor do they invite roads and you soon find that your trackway is resolved to leave this formidable moel well to the right.

Where the road ventures across slopes you see that it is carefully

A Bronze Age circle on Bryn Cader Faner in the Rhinog range between Harlech and Trawsfynydd

supported by boulders. Elsewhere you find it has been cut through rock or paved across marshland and with an effort you can picture horse-drawn vehicles bumping across these empty moors. For this ancient trackway's final use, before man abandoned it at last, was as a coaching road. You reach a point where the road swings boldly right towards Llyn Eiddew-bach. But this is a modern aberration to be avoided. The ancient road goes straight on with a wall on its left, eventually missing the lake by a few hundred yards, passing first a stone circle, then a ruined cairn some sixty yards on. From here through binoculars you can see the prize exhibit of this walk – the stone circle conspicuous on the hill called Bryn Cader Faner (SH 648353). This was one of the best pre-served of all the Park's Bronze Age monuments until about 1940 when it was vandalised by soldiers on wartime exercises. Until then it had endured as a complete circle of about thirty stones all leaning outwards in the position in which their builders had set them. And though half the stones have now gone it is still a most attractive little cairn circle.

From here the coach road struggles on across the moors and bogs, keeping high for as long as it can. Then it leaps into the wild hollow of Cwm Moch, crosses a stream and goes clambering with determination up the other side, here and there well built on supporting stones. That we are still on the Bronze Age route is implied by the hoard of four bronze rapiers (hidden by a merchant?) found here soon after 1800, carefully tucked away in a space under a boulder. The next evidence is a stocky little standing stone called Maen Llwyd (SH 707329) a mile or so south of Trawsfynydd and 400 yards west of the main road along a farm track. Then another 2 miles south-east is Llech Idris (SH 731311), a commanding stone standing alone in a field and hinting that the route continued on to the Bala region (where there are more Bronze Age remains) and so on towards south-east England.

South of the Mawddach estuary other Bronze Age routes may have gone inland from the mouth of the Dysynni, now (like the Artro) a silted estuary but in those days perhaps a good harbour. One conjecture is that a road went north to Llwyngwril then, by way of a sequence of still surviving standing stones, passed over the hills and down to join Ffordd Ddu ('the black road') which skirts round the north of Cader Idris and then off to the east. A torc (ornamental collar) made of Bronze Age Irish gold, found long ago between Cader and Dolgellau, had probably been hidden by some traveller along this road.

Another immemorial route, which also links with Ffordd Ddu, goes from Aberdysynni past the old church of Llanegryn and makes a bold north-easterly line up the valley of the Afon Gwril near whose head it

Standing stones and other Bronze Age remains are a special feature of the coastal
regions of the Park. This monolith is near the ancient road, Ffordd Ddu, nearly a
mile south-west of Cregennen Lakes. The slopes of Tyrau Mawr near Cader Idris
rise in the background

is joined by yet another age-old road that comes up from Peniarth and has superb glimpses back across the Dysynni valley to Bird Rock. Among the best of the standing stones near the line of Ffordd Ddu are those at SH 626117, SH 651133 and SH 661138, this last one, called Carreg y Big, being just south of the Cregennen Lakes. Archaeology apart, all these stones are well worth visiting for their far views across this ancient Mawddach landscape.

The Iron Age

Something like five centuries before the coming of the Romans the first Celtic tribes settled in Britain bringing with them a knowledge of iron and an end to the Bronze Age. They also brought a language which was a precursor of Welsh and which survives even in England in a few place-names. The most visible relics of the Iron Age are the many hill forts, among the best of which in Snowdonia are: Caer Leion on Conwy Mountain (SH 760778); Pen-y-gaer in the Conwy valley (SH 750693); Dinas Dinorwig near Llanberis (SH 549653); Dinas Emrys near Beddgelert (SH 606492); Moel Goedog near Harlech (SH 613325); Craig y Dinas (SH 624230) and Pen y Dinas (SH 606209), both near Dyffryn Ardudwy; Bryn-y-castell near Ffestiniog (SH 728429); Moel Offrwm near Dolgellau (SH 750210); and Craig yr Aderyn near Tywyn (SH 643067).

In some of the hill forts, as on Conwy Mountain, you will see the foundations of circular huts but nowhere in the Park have they survived so lavishly as at Tre'r Ceiri ('town of the giants'), a marvellous fort on Yr Eifl (SH 373446) 13 miles south-west of Caernarfon. The Park's hut circles, some single, some grouped within enclosures and sited near terraced fields, are often known locally as *cytiau'r Gwyddelod* ('Irish-men's huts'). They are most abundant in the north and west, especially on slopes not far from the sea. The further you go inland the fewer you find. Maps often mark them as 'Settlement' or 'Field System'. They can be found on the slopes above Cwm Pennant and Cwmystradllyn north of Cricieth, and also in the country from Cnicht and Moelwyn to the hills above Cardigan Bay.

Celtic field outlines are particularly well preserved above Dyffryn Ardudwy and southwards towards Barmouth. An enclosure of huts with adjacent fields is well known just above Harlech as Muriau'r Gwyddelod ('Irishmen's walls') (SH 586301). The site is close to the Bronze Age route to Trawsfynydd and if you pursue this track as far as Cwm Moch (SH 665362) you will see, where it comes down to the stream, the wall bases of two circular rooms of an enclosed homestead. (Three rectangular rooms adjacent to them may be a medieval addition.) It has been suggested that the most likely purpose of a house in such a remote and unliveable spot was as a wayside inn. But the interpretation and dating of many of the settlements and hill forts is often very uncertain because their total period of occupation extended from long before to long after the Roman period.

Roman times

It was probably in quest of metals that the Romans thought it worth their while to occupy Snowdonia and they did it with characteristic efficiency, quickly setting up a well-planned system of strongholds and roads. Their major centre, founded about AD78, was Segontium, whose remains you can see on the south-eastern outskirts of Caernarfon along A4085 (the Beddgelert road) which cuts across the site of the fort. Much of Segontium has been thoroughly excavated. It is open to the public and there is an excellent museum. Fragments of Roman walls survive but the rest of the stones were carried off long ago, especially in the thirteenth century, to build Caernarfon Castle and the town walls. That Segontium remained a Roman fortress for three hundred years (though probably not continuously) is attested by the long series of coins and other finds the site has yielded.

Roman forts of less importance in the Park were at Canovium (Caerhun) (SH 776703), a delightful spot close to the tidal Conwy and now partly occupied by a medieval church; at Tomen-y-mur (SH 706386) near Trawsfynydd and easily picked out by the large castle mound (a contribution of the Middle Ages) that you see on the skyline as you pass along A470 near the nuclear power-station; at Cefn-caer (SH 705001) which commanded the Dyfi estuary near Pennal; and at Caer Gai (SH 877314) near Bala. Among other Roman sites are Bryncir (SH 481449) 11 miles south of Caernarfon; Tremadog (SH 557401); Caer Llugwy or Bryn-y-gefeiliau (SH 746572), in a field on the banks of the river between Capel Curig and Betws-y-coed; Pen-y-gwryd (SH 660557); and Brithdir (SH 771188) near Dolgellau. Apart from Segontium and Canovium we do not know what names the Romans gave to their forts in Snowdonia.

A few Roman milestones (for instance between Caernarfon and Caerhun) have survived and are now in museums. But most Roman roads lack authentication. In some areas their courses are fairly clear, in others highly conjectural. The best known are Caernarfon to

Caerhun via Bwlch y Ddeufaen; Caerhun to Tomen-y-mur; Caernarfon to Caer Gai (Bala) by way of Bryncir, Tremadog and Tomen-y-mur; Tomen-y-mur to Dolgellau; and Dolgellau to Caer Gai. But it is only here and there that even these best-known roads have been proved by the spade to be undoubtedly Roman. Still unknown are the whereabouts of the fort (if any) at Dolgellau and the course of the road from Dolgellau to Pennal. Did it go east, west or over the top of the Cader Idris ridge?

'Sarn Elen' (or 'Helen') is an ancient name still given to several Roman roads including the one coming down through Snowdonia from Caerhun to Pennal and on into south Wales. It is probably an invention of that branch of folklore which did its imaginative best to explain mysterious place-names. In the *Mabinogion* the story called 'The Dream of Macsen Wledig' relates that Elen was the Welsh wife of an obscure Roman emperor, Maximus (Macsen in Welsh), and that it was through her influence that a great programme of road improvements was put into effect: 'And for that reason they are called the Roads of Elen.' 'Sarn', meaning a paved way, is often associated with Welsh Roman roads and a likely derivation of 'Sarn Elen' is from some hypothetical name like *Sarn y Leng*, meaning 'the paved way of the legions'. Among the more convincing fragments of Roman roads are those along Sarn Helen 2 miles south-east of Blaenau Ffestiniog, from the edge of the forestry plantations at SH 738453 south to Rhyd yr Helen (Helen's Ford) at SH 729433.

The Dark Ages

Little enough has survived from the Roman period but we have even less to show for the shadowy centuries that followed, although they must have been a crucial formative period when the social patterns of the Middle Ages began to be established. There is a tissue of legends involving figures like Arthur, Merlin, Vortigern and others who belong to the twilight world between fiction and reality. But when we try to picture the actualities of their daily lives, all we have is a vague background of the hill forts that continued in use after the Romans had gone and of the hut circles, settlements and field outlines which have been assigned, with some uncertainty, to the Dark Ages. It was a time when Christianity was steadily spreading in the steps of the holy men of the fifth, sixth and seventh centuries who founded the early churches. The simple wooden structures they created have gone but we can feel sure that many of the sites have survived and are now marked by medieval churches which still remember the names of their founders, good Celtic names such as Cadfan, Tanwg, Tydecho, Peblig and Celynin.

Tangible remains of the early Celtic Church are the inscribed slabs, nearly all of them gravestones with lettering in Latin. Preserved in many churches and museums their message is usually quite clear. *Carausius hic jacit in hoc congeries lapidum*, says one of the stones in Penmachno church ('In this pile of stones Carausius lies buried'). Over in the west, on a slab in Llanaber church, *Caelexti monedo rigi* is more tricky but probably means '[The stone] of Caelextus Monedorix'. That a famous stone in Tywyn church has so far defied translation is most regrettable because it is thought to be the oldest specimen of written Welsh. It is also sad that no great carved crosses have survived in Snowdonia to compare with those elsewhere in Wales.

The Middle Ages

In and around Snowdonia the medieval time speaks to us most eloquently through its castles and churches. The castles are mostly those which the conquering English set up in the days of Edward I as an

Now one of the remotest bridges in Snowdonia, Pont Scethin carried an old moorland road that linked Bont Ddu on the Mawddach estuary with the coast near Dyffryn Ardudwy

unbreakable chain stretched round the north and west. Though now mainly empty shells, their outer walls still stand high; and enough of their interiors survive to enable us to understand the thinking behind their construction. Beginning in the east these great castles are at Conwy, Beaumaris, Caernarfon, Cricieth and Harlech, the coastal line being completed by two that are well outside the Park at Rhuddlan in the north-east and Aberystwyth in the south-west.

Of all these thirteenth-century castles Caernarfon is the most celebrated. With its many tall towers and high walls it truly is a princely building, especially when seen with the tidal water in front of it and the mountains behind. It is also cherished for its scenes of pageantry such as the investiture of the princes of Wales. Linked with the castle are the substantially intact town walls which enclosed the medieval borough and are an important example of urban fortification of about 1300. Conwy Castle too is completely magnificent and has the added glory of medieval town walls which are much more extensive even than those at Caernarfon. Beyond the Menai Strait, Beaumaris Castle, rather less grand and never quite completed, is interesting for its ingenious construction and is most attractively moated. Perched on their high rocks Harlech and Cricieth castles look at each other across 7 miles of sea. All these castles are open to the public and information about them is available on the site.

Inland, three lesser fortresses are also open to visitors. Dolbadarn Castle, beautifully placed at the edge of Llyn Peris, a mile south-east of Llanberis, was a Welsh castle probably created by Llywelyn the Great. Dolwyddelan Castle, conspicuous on a hill above A470 5 miles south-west of Betws-y-coed, was also built by the Welsh but was captured and strengthened by Edward I. Castell y Bere, 7 miles up the Dysynni valley from Tywyn, had a similar fate. But it is a castle you need to rebuild in your imagination because nothing remains of it except the stumps of its walls. Around it Edward hoped to build a town but the plan never got far beyond the drawing-board and even after seven hundred years there are still only green fields and hills all round. Botanists enjoy this castle because it is built on rocks lime-rich enough to grow marjoram, orpine, tutsan and other plants not all that common in Snowdonia.

Medieval churches

In the Middle Ages Snowdonia had two Cistercian abbeys: at Conwy (founded 1172) and at Cymer near Dolgellau (1199). Conwy Abbey was eventually moved 8 miles up the estuary to Maenan by Edward I to make room for his new castle; and all that survives of it at Conwy are fragments in the structure of St Mary's church. The replacement abbey at Maenan stood until the Dissolution but nothing is now left above ground. Its rood screen and loft went to Llanrwst church and are still there. The abbey at Cymer (SH 7219) has fared a little better. It has largely disappeared but parts of the church walls remain, including three good arches on the north side. It is close to the banks of the Mawddach near a fine old bridge and is open to the public.

Most of the Park's medieval churches are buildings with only slight architectural pretensions and a few, like Llangelynnin (SH 571071) on the sea cliffs north of Tywyn, are simplicity itself. Usually the churches still have their communities gathered closely around them. But Llanegryn church (near Tywyn) stands apart, high above the modern village. And from a few churches human life has drained even more completely away, leaving them to the loneliness of the hills. You will find that this

Pont Minllyn, an early seventeenth century packhorse bridge over the Dyfi at Dinas Mawddwy. It was built by Dr John Davies, parish rector and eminent Welsh scholar

has happened to two of the most primitive Conwy valley churches: Llangelynnin (SH 752737) and Llanrhychwyn (SH 775616). For information about other old churches see the Gazetteer.

Later centuries

The post-medieval centuries survive in many forms. But the ephemeral homes of the poor have mostly vanished. So too have whole communities like the one which flourished (or failed to flourish) at Ardda on the moorland shelf above Dolgarrôg in the Conwy valley. More substantial dwellings, especially farmhouses, are still inhabited though centuries old, and sometimes their outbuildings are older still as you can see from the carpentry of their roofs. Here and there you will find a farmhouse that has clearly evolved from the traditional long-house where the farmers and their cattle all lived under one roof and were separated only by a door.

Today's inhabited farmhouses are nearly all in the lowlands; but up on the moorlands you will meet with abandoned houses in every stage of decay. They remember a time (it lasted until early this century) when people stocked up with food in the autumn and spent the winter in near solitude, isolated by snowdrifts and quags. In any district it would be a worthwhile project to plot these old homesteads on maps before they all disappear under the turf, as some must have done already. In the villages and small towns of the lowlands there is a scattering of old cottages and houses; and along the streams are the ruins of corn mills, fulling mills (pandy in Welsh) and weaving mills – all memories of a vanished way of life.

Most of the towns have retained at least a few houses whose styles reflect not only the different periods of architecture but also various types of local building stone, most of them slates, shales or granites. The country seats of the gentry, rarely on a grand scale, are scattered throughout the Park, many of them now converted to hotel or other uses. Among houses of interest and open to the public are: Gwydir Castle near Llanrwst; Plas Mawr and Aberconwy House, both in Conwy; and Penrhyn Castle, Bangor. A cheerful whimsey of modern architecture is the Italian-style village of Portmeirion near Penrhyndeudraeth. (For further information on old houses consult the Gazetteer.)

When built in the thirteenth century Harlech Castle had the sea at its feet but land has accreted since then and the sea is now half a mile away

Old roads

The history of roads – almost the longest of human stories – can be quite indecipherable, so often have the passing generations obliterated the tracks of their predecessors. It is on the uplands that we find the old ways best preserved – the bridle paths, coaching routes and drovers' roads that struggled over hills unacceptable to modern traffic. As you follow these superseded roads you will sometimes see how different centuries have had their own ideas about how to get across a valley or through a pass and have left traces of their routes staged one above the other across the slopes. In almost every valley and mountain pass you will find examples of old roads in all stages of preservation. Some are still very well defined like the one along the south side of Nant Ffrancon; many others are shadowy fragments slowly vanishing from history.

Old bridges

Many of Snowdonia's rivers and streams are crossed by stone bridges that are centuries old. Some are multi-arched like Llanelltyd Bridge over the Mawddach, Dolgellau Bridge over the Wnion, Bryncrug Bridge over the Dysynni and Machynlleth Bridge over the Dyfi. Far commoner are the single-arched but very substantial bridges that carry the roads over narrower waters. Often they are an attractive feature of wooded gorges as you will find especially around Betws-y-coed. Seldom does a bridge have a date carved on it and even if it does the reference may be only to the year of a repair.

On the moorlands you may come upon smaller bridges which carried lighter traffic and were unlikely to have to face the huge floods which have so often swept away bridges down in the lowlands where all waters gather. One such upland bridge is Pont Scethin near Talybont (SH 635235) which was used by coaches; another, a gem of a pack-horse bridge, is Pont Llaeron above Abergynolwyn (SH 701049).

More than one bridge is called 'Roman' but this is only a courtesy title for anything thought to be ancient. Here and there, however, along the Roman roads you may come upon the abutments of former bridges that may have been truly Roman work, eg on Sarn Helen near Ffestiniog where it crosses Nant Drewi, a rivulet near Carreg-y-fran.

The Idwal Slabs in Cwm Idwal on the Glyder range are a popular 'nursery' for climbers

Field walls

Stone walls enclosing huge fields and stretching right over the mountain tops have a huge impact on the scenery. The early nineteenth century was probably the greatest wall-building period, though John Leland remarked on the walls even in early Tudor times. After the Napoleonic War the enclosure movement was going on apace and in that time of social distress labour was very cheap. T. P. Ellis, in his history of the Dolgellau area, tells us:

> The result of the enclosures was a great change in the landscape and from the period date the great stone fences . . .. Sir Robert Vaughan is credited with building fifty-five miles of walls and he maintained nine carters and eighteen horses or mules.

Today we accept these remarkable walls as an attractive landscape feature. They are also invaluable habitats for lichens, wheatears, weasels, stoats and polecats. Perhaps our chief regret about them might be that their builders thought fit to plunder or destroy so many cairns and other ancient monuments. As well as fine upstanding walls, mostly kept in good repair, you will also come upon the stumps of walls that are clearly far more ancient. Undatable, they could go back to any moment in the human story.

6
THE INDUSTRIAL PAST

Whilst I and three gentlemen who happened to be with me the day I visited the mine, were watching the women break ore, a loaded waggon was brought out of the level. This gave us an opportunity of returning in an empty one to examine the interior of the work. We therefore leaped into the waggon and, with one miner before to drag and two others behind to push us along, we entered the narrow cavern . . . . The day was one of those excessively hot ones that we frequently have about the middle of August; and the chilling damp which immediately struck us on entering, added not a little to the terrors of the place . . . . When we came to the end of the level we got out of the waggon and, each lighting his candle, followed our guides into a cavern so high that all our lights did not render the roof visible . . . .

So, in the summer of 1801, did the Reverend William Bingley seize the chance of getting into the copper mine at Llanberis. On his visit to Snowdonia, Bingley's main interest was botany but it was typical of the touring gentry of those days never to miss a chance of inspecting the deafening mills, the darksome mines and the roaring furnaces of industry; and in their highly emotional descriptions of them they made as much as possible out of the terror, gloom and horror of everything they saw. Theirs was a generation enchanted by the romance of industry (the poet Shelley was wildly in favour of the new embankment at Porthmadog even though it destroyed a beautiful estuary) and it was not until later in the nineteenth century, when the Industrial Revolution had lost its novelty, that people began to count the cost of it all in terms of human misery and sprawls of shoddy housing.

Snowdonia has been so thoroughly explored for stone or metals since the earliest times that there is scarcely a hillside that has not been dug into at some time by hopeful prospectors. Very few of these trial holes ever brought success but some of those which did develop into mines or quarries have left huge scars on the scene. Today the metal mines are all derelict except for a couple of small gold mines; and even many of the great quarries for slate and roadstone are silent.

The quarries

Of all these industries none has had an impact on the landscape anything like as great as that of the quarries. The extraction of igneous rock which still goes on at Penmaenmawr has entirely removed the mountain summit (and with it one of Snowdonia's best hill forts complete with many hut circles). There are also huge quarry scars in similar rocks in the sea cliffs at Trefor, south-west of Caernarfon, and on the north side of Arennig Fawr. Yet even these wounds are far less than those of some of the slate quarries. So it is not surprising that the main slate-producing areas – Nantlle, Llanberis, Bethesda, Blaenau Ffestiniog and Corris – were carefully excluded when the Park's limits were defined.

The most spectacular quarries are in rocks of Cambrian age on opposite flanks of Elidir Fawr. On the west side, facing Llanberis, is the Dinorwig (or Dinorwic) quarry which goes up the mountainside in regular horizontal terraces which were worked simultaneously. Unlike Dinorwig quarry, which sprawls across an open slope, the Bethesda workings, on the eastern slopes of Elidir, are cut into the hillside in the shape of a horseshoe. Otherwise the size of terracing and methods of working were similar in the two quarries.

These slate-bearing Cambrian rocks extend in a narrow belt about eleven miles long from Bethesda south-west through Elidir to Llanberis and on to the Nantlle area. But at Nantlle they are less a feature of hillsides, most of them lying deep in the valley bottom. So here much of the slate was won by digging holes which, as the years went by, became immensely long, wide and deep. This type of extraction was not as easy as quarrying on mountainside terraces and it also had problems with flooding. Among the most famous quarries at Nantlle were the Dorothea and the Pen-yr-orsedd.

The rocks of the next age, the Ordovician, also yield high-quality slates, chiefly at Blaenau Ffestiniog. Here much of the slate lies deep inside the mountains and has to be mined rather than quarried. And just as Dinorwig claimed to be the world's biggest slate quarry so Blaenau claims to have the world's biggest slate mines. They consist of a series of underground chambers up to 120ft (36m) long, 40ft (12m) wide and 100ft (30m) high with pillars left at intervals to support the roof. They lie one below the other down to fifteen different levels, so reaching 1,500ft (460m) in total depth. All around the Ffestiniog region you will come upon abandoned quarries. Many were small and unprofitable; a few were immensely wealthy and kept hundreds of people in employment for many years. Also in the Ordovician rocks there were important slate quarries at Dolwyddelan and Penmachno, and in the south of the Park at Arthog, Abergynolwyn, Aberllefenni and Corris. South of Corris we leave the Ordovician for the Silurian but the disused quarries continue down to Machynlleth and beyond, one of them now the home of the Centre for Alternative Technology.

No doubt man has been roofing with Snowdonia's slate since the very first houses were built here, for such easily-split rock, producing thin yet strong and waterproof sheets, could not have escaped attention. The earliest attested use of it dates from the Roman fort of Segontium at Caernarfon where purple slates went into the flooring as well as the roofing. Slate was extensively used in the Middle Ages in building the castles and new towns of Caernarfon and Conwy, and there is a record of it being exported to Ireland in the sixteenth century. But down the centuries the slate came from small local sources and it was not until the late eighteenth and early nineteenth centuries that large-scale quarrying began. This was when the owners of large estates, instead of leasing their land to groups of small-scale entrepreneurs who were part-time farmers, part-time slate-workers, began to develop their own much grander quarrying enterprises. This happened most spectacularly at Dinorwig under the lord of the manor, Assheton Smith, and at Bethesda under Lord Penrhyn. With this new regime the quarries made great technical advances, roads were built to carry the slates to the outside world (for example, Lord Penrhyn's road which preceded Telford's through Nant Ffrancon), and narrow-gauge railways linked the Bethesda and Dinorwig quarries with their ports on the Menai Strait.

The greatest days were the second and third quarters of the nineteenth century when some of the proprietors made vast fortunes. During the last quarter a decline set in: it was a period of increasing foreign competition and there was a gradual development of cheaper roofing materials, the difficulties being added to by bitter industrial dis-

The abandoned Dinorwig slate quarry above Llyn Peris on the slopes of Elidir Fawr. The lake is now the lower reservoir of a pumped storage hydro-electric power station whose machinery is concealed in caverns under the mountain

putes. The first half of the twentieth century saw the industry struggling on and just surviving the depression of the thirties. There were a few brief bursts of prosperity but then even the greatest quarries began to close down one after another. Dinorwig, for instance, finished in 1969.

Though many of the old metal mines may now be quite hard to find, there is no missing a slate quarry no matter how long abandoned (with the exception of those now engulfed by conifers). Slate quarries and mines are proclaimed by the vast quantities of rock which had to be moved and dumped to get at the high-quality product required by the market. Sometimes as much as twenty tons of what to the uninitiated looks like good slate had to be wasted to achieve one ton of saleable material.

Slate tips are not beautiful. Nor do they readily clothe themselves with vegetation. The few which happen to have enough soil mixed in with them, or lying just under them, eventually green over, often with birches. But the majority remain bare (except for lichens) or at best acquire a little parsley fern or woolly-haired moss. Certainly any plants that aspire to colonise a tip or a quarry face need to be able to manage without lime, for slate is limeless stuff.

In 1967 at Aberfan in south Wales a huge coal tip suddenly slipped down a mountainside and buried a school and a generation of children. It was a tragedy which alerted people to the dangers of tips of all kinds and in north Wales some of the more precarious heaps of slate waste were removed. One of the biggest schemes was at Corris where slate spoil had long threatened the main road from the steep slopes above. Between upper and lower Corris, near the present craft centre, the tips and disused buildings were entirely relandscaped and the road was rerouted down the centre of the valley.

Many of the old slate workings are sited far into the loneliness of the hills where one hopes they will long be quiet refuges for kestrels, choughs, stock doves and other creatures. Today it is not always easy to picture how these mines and quarries operated. For apart from their tips and their sometimes huge excavations there is often very little left of their buildings and still less of their machinery. It is in response to the ever-growing public interest in industrial archaeology that the very popular visitor centres have been developed at the Llanberis and Blaenau Ffestiniog quarries.

At Llanberis the end of Padarn Lake is now a country park with waterside picnic places and 2 miles of lakeside narrow-gauge railway. But the major interest here is the slate industry. You can plod slowly or leap gazelle-like along trails that take you steeply up and over the great gash in the hillside which was the Vivian quarry. Like all the Dinorwig quarries it rises in gigantic steps up the side of Elidir Fawr. It was carved last century out of a wooded slope and in the years since work ceased, the oaks, rowans and birches have reclaimed much of the lost ground; and as you go up the trails in spring the trees are full of the songs of redstarts, wood warblers, pied flycatchers and other birds. Large wood ants – food for the many green woodpeckers – scurry over the ground and climb high up the trees.

A trail leaflet guides you up through the quarry, explaining step by step: the old quarry hospital complete with primitive medical equipment; the working face (now an occasional playground for rock-climbers); the slate-dressing areas; the inclines and winding houses; a double row of ruined barracks remarkable for their tall chimneys; and as a final reward you get a superb view from the top to all the mountains, including Snowdon. Down at lake level is the Slate Museum, an outstation of the National Museum of Wales that is housed in workshops of unusual magnificence built in 1870. Here you learn that the Dinorwig quarries

111

once employed over three thousand men and produced tens of thousands of tons of roofing slates annually which were shipped all over the world.

The museum retains much of the original machinery along with a smithy, a foundry, steam locomotives, rolling stock and much information about the quarry's history. A prize exhibit is one of Britain's largest waterwheels. It once powered all the machinery and still turns with elegant smoothness as water pours on to it from above. The country park includes the Vivian quarry only. For those who want to visit the whole vast range of the Dinorwig quarries small groups can arrange to be taken round on land-rover safaris organised by the museum.

In contrast with the open mountainside quarries at Llanberis and Bethesda are the slate mines at Blaenau Ffestiniog. If you follow A470 up the hill towards Betws-y-coed you will find these spectacular workings are open to the public on either side of the road. First comes Llechwedd on the right, then Gloddfa Ganol on the left. You are taken far down into these chilly mines, either on foot or by train, and everything to do with the slate industry is revealed with suitable lighting and sound effects. At the surface are workshops and exhibitions relating to the whole history of the industry and its workers. Serious slate extraction began here at the start of the nineteenth century and took a hundred years to reach its peak, the Blaenau population rising during that time from 700 to over 11,000. This century has seen a decline to below 6,000 people and very few of them are employed by the slate industry. But lately there has been a modest increase in the demand for quality slate, so perhaps we are about to see a revival in this industry which over two centuries has so often had to face the slings and arrows of trade depressions.

Copper mining

Man and copper have long been acquainted. The metal was smelted in Egypt as long ago as about 4000BC and its use in Britain goes back to about 1800BC with the arrival of the Bronze Age people (bronze being an alloy of copper and tin). The likelihood is that there were already copper mines in north-west Wales before the Romans reached here in their determined pursuit of minerals. Certainly there was mining during the Roman time, for several of their copper cakes, some stamped in Latin, have been found. Most have been picked up in Anglesey and no doubt came from the mine on Parys Mountain near Amlwch. The Great Orme at Llandudno is also reckoned to have had Roman copper mines. And within the Snowdonia Park the most ancient, perhaps pre-historic, mines may be those on Snowdon and in Aberglaslyn Pass.

There have been many copper mines in Snowdonia, nearly all small, a lot of them little more than trial holes. Most date from the eighteenth and especially the nineteenth centuries. A few carried on until the twentieth but all are at present abandoned. Many can still be located by their spoil heaps but their machinery has nearly all gone, their buildings are mostly fragmentary or vanished, their shafts and levels sometimes hard to find. Among the best known or most interesting, besides those on Snowdon and in Aberglaslyn Pass, were the mines at Drws-y-coed in the Nantlle Valley; on the southern slopes of Lliwedd above Nant Gwynant; above the south side of Llyn Peris in Llanberis Pass; at Sygun, a mile east of Beddgelert; in Cwm Bychan, Nantmor; at Glasdir, 4 miles north of Dolgellau; and at Ynysmaengwyn near Tywyn. The erudite study by David Bick, *The Old Copper Mines of Snowdonia* (1982), is a marvellous history of the mines north of the Vale of Ffestiniog. But as the author points out, much remains to be unearthed about many of them.

There is an air of romance today about these old mines but it is well not to forget what dreadful places they were to work in. Both underground and in the crushing sheds, conditions were often appallingly cold, wet and miserable; there was the ever-present threat of accidents and metal poisoning; and the barracks the men stayed in were wretched. In the early years of Snowdon's Glaslyn mine, before there was a road through Llanberis Pass, the ore used to be carried on men's backs up the side of Snowdon from Llyn Glaslyn to the summit ridge. It was then sledged down by horses to the Caernarfon road near what is now the Snowdon Ranger youth hostel, formerly the Saracen's Head hotel. Just one sentence from David Bick's account of the early days of this mine says enough about the working conditions: 'In the winter of 1801 the miners had to cut a tunnel through snow to reach the level, the drifts being up to 20 yards deep in many places.'

Probably not many of the entrepreneurs got rich from their mining activities. Yet despite many losses and failures there seldom seems to have been a shortage of new speculators ready to have a gamble, ever eager to believe the extravagant claims made by promoters and agents about the wonderful prospects offered by practically every trial hole in Snowdonia. For instance in a report on a trial level on Moel Hebog in the 1850s it was claimed that 'as the side of the land was perpendicular they had only, as it were, to open a door and take the copper out . . .. It appeared to be an entire mountain of copper'.

113

Copper is still widespread in the Park but the breadth and extent of its lodes are very haphazard; nowhere does the ore seem very rich and even the most promising veins have soon petered out. It was the discovery of much vaster and richer sources of copper abroad which brought mining to a halt in Wales. But if the world price of copper were to rise high enough we can be sure that the exploiters would soon be back, as in 1971 when Rio Tinto Zinc came prospecting for copper near Capel Hermon north-east of Dolgellau.

Naturalists have long been attracted by the old copper mines as likely breeding places for choughs, barn owls, stock doves, bats and other troglodytes. And botanists are aware of an odd little group of plants that especially enjoy copper mine spoil heaps though copper is generally poisonous to vegetation. Spring sandwort flourishes on the tips at Capel Hermon and in Llanberis Pass. At Hermon it is accompanied by quantities of sea campion and thrift which, though typical seaside plants, also flourish in limy places on mountains. Probably they are attracted to the mine tips by the presence of calcium carbonate, a common constituent of mineral-bearing lodes. Also near Hermon is the well-known Dôl-frwynog peat bog (SH 745255) where over a long period copper sulphate has dissolved out of the local rocks and impregnated the ground. The peat when burnt yielded copper ore rich enough to be shipped off to Swansea for refining in the early nineteenth century.

Lead mines

If man's knowledge of lead is not quite as old as that of copper it certainly goes back to the ancient world and by classical times lead had become an accepted part of civilised life. When they got to Britain the Romans were eager in its quest, one of their chief uses of it being the making of water pipes. Little did they suspect they were poisoning the water supplies of generations to come. As with the copper mines it seems likely that lead mines already existed in Wales before the Romans arrived on the scene. After all, copper and lead ores often occur close to each other and a people who knew the use of one would soon have learnt to recognise and process the other.

Other metals, especially zinc and silver, are often found with lead, and down the centuries they too were turned to account. In fact there were periods when the lead-zinc mines were nothing but silver mines, the base metals being wasted. Certainly all mining has alternated between comparatively short bursts of activity and much longer periods of neglect, so long that sometimes the mines have been quite lost and forgotten. Lead mines (none now operating) are widespread in Wales and especially abundant in the old counties of Cardigan, Montgomery and Flint. In Snowdonia lead was of rather less importance than copper except in the region immediately north of Betws-y-coed between the Carneddau and the Conwy river. Here there were about a score of mines working mainly from the mid-nineteenth century until World War I. After that lead from the United States and elsewhere put Welsh lead out of business.

Until this century the Betws-y-coed lead district was a land of open moorland scattered with little lakes and mine reservoirs. But it has been transformed by the Forestry Commission into a world of conifers amongst which the pools and the mine remains are rather hidden. Some of the spoil heaps are still devoid of vegetation but the less poisonous ones have been successfully planted with trees or have been colonised by wild plants among which are two very local species: alpine pennycress and the strange little fern called forked spleenwort. This miniature lake district is centred on a conifer-clad upland called Mynydd Bwlch-yr-haiarn and is traversed by the narrow but motorable lane that leaves A5 at the Ugly House (Tŷ Hyll) and winds through the forest either to Llyn Geirionydd or down to near Gwydir Castle, passing close to two well-known mines on its way: Parc (SH 788602) and Hafna (SH 781601).

Among the many small lead mines elsewhere in the Park (besides innumerable trial holes that came to nothing) were those at Trecastell, 3 miles south-west of Conwy; Moelwyn Bach, west of Blaenau Ffestiniog and at the Gamallt lakes to the east; Bwlch-y-plwm (*plwm* means lead), Llanfrothen; Llanllyfni in the Nantlle valley; Cwm-hesian near Llanfachreth; Moel Isbri and others along the Dolgellau gold belt; Cywarch near Dinas Mawddwy and others at Tywyn and Aberdyfi.

Manganese mines

It is in the Rhinog range that manganese ore (pyrolusite) has been chiefly mined in the Park, though it was at one time exploited at Sygun copper mine east of Beddgelert and in the Arennig range near Bala. The Rhinog area is believed to hold large quantities of manganese ore but it is of such poor quality that the mines (worked mainly in the late nineteenth and early twentieth centuries) were all short-lived, leaving little to show except a few levels, open-cast workings and causeways.

There were mines near Harlech, on Moelfre mountain near Llanbedr, in the Nantcol valley at Maes-y-garnedd and on the east side of

Diffwys above the Mawddach estuary. This last site is now one of the best known because its old tramway has become a popular route up Diffwys from Cwm Mynach (between Bont Ddu and Dolgellau). The tramway begins in a forestry plantation and although it disappears for long stretches you can pick it up intermittently all the way up to the mine. Indeed some sections of it are in remarkably good condition.

Manganese, so vital to the steel industry and with many other uses, is available in vast amounts in various parts of the world and is unlikely to be mined in Wales except in an emergency.

Naturalists do not seem to have reported any plants or animals certainly associated with manganese. But, sited as they are in the limeless Cambrian rocks, the mines are often deep in heather and other calcifuges, and if you go up there on a fine May day when the bilberries are in flower you will find them visited by bilberry bumble bees which are distinctive for their red-brown tails. A local little fern, lanceolate spleenwort, found near Barmouth, could possibly be linked with the presence of managanese but there is no proof of this.

Gold mines

Although gold, usually in the form of invisible, scattered grains or more rarely as flakes, is widespread in the world's igneous rocks, the celebrated gold of Snowdonia has not generally been found in the Ordovician igneous outcrops which form the bulk of the Park's rocks. Instead it occurs mainly in the Cambrian rocks on the south and south-east slopes of the Harlech Dome. Gold is reckoned to have been carried up from great depths with other minerals in solution and in Snowdonia is found in veins of quartz as you can see from the predominance of quartz in the spoil heaps of the mines.

The Dolgellau gold-belt stretches from near Bont-ddu north-east to the upper reaches of the Mawddach. Above Bont-ddu the best-known mines are Vigra, St Davids and Clogau; in the north-east there is Gwynfynydd mine, close to the waterfalls of Pistyll Cain and Rhaeadr Mawddach. As well as these the district is riddled with trial excavations, the result of spasmodic outbursts of gold fever. Outside the Dolgellau areas but still in Cambrian rocks of the Harlech Dome, gold has been found nearly three miles north-east of Trawsfynydd (Prince Edward mine) and in nearby Cwm Prysor. One mine stands apart from the Harlech Dome: it was at Castell Carndochan, 6 miles south-west of Bala, and was in Ordovician rocks.

The Romans are sometimes said to have known about Mawddach

gold but the evidence is flimsy. Modern interest certainly dates back no earlier than the 1840s. There followed about twenty years of activity, then twenty years of doldrums before a revival began in the 1880s. This century has seen sporadic bursts of enthusiasm which still continue from time to time. During their brief peaks the best mines were very profitable but although gold is still thought to exist in some quantity it is extremely difficult to locate and its extraction is very expensive. But being the mind-turning metal it is, gold will no doubt go on tempting speculators even in Snowdonia's unpromising rocks. For the past century a few optimists have, with very mild success, panned for gold in the Mawddach river and still do so, picking up here and there a yellow flake. It must be rather like fishing in an almost fishless river. There is probably gold also in the mud of the Mawddach estuary: or so Rio Tinto Zinc thought in 1971 when they made their short-lived dredging proposals.

Roads and bridges

In or near the Park there are several famous roads and bridges of enormous interest to industrial archaeologists. Telford's elegant suspension bridge crossed the Menai Strait close to Bangor in 1826, one of the last and most difficult links he had to make between London and Dublin. When complete it was one of the wonders of the age and much written about. An excellent contemporary description of it can be found in William Cathrall's *History of North Wales* (1828) which also has a fine drawing of this bridge as well as of Telford's other masterpiece, the Conwy suspension bridge, which he built as part of the coastal road towards Chester (now A55). Telford's great inland road to Bangor came from Shrewsbury by way of Capel Curig and Nant Ffrancon. Where it crossed the Conwy at Betws-y-coed he built his famous iron arch, the Waterloo Bridge (1815) which still carries the main road. (A5).

Standard-gauge railways

The revolution in communications which Telford helped to bring about was fated to be short-lived. Only twenty-five years later his roads were largely superseded by the new railways and again the crossing of the Conwy estuary and the Menai Strait called for an engineering genius, this time Stephenson, who solved the problems at both sites by his tubular bridges which, though lacking the beauty of Telford's creations, proved to be immensely strong. The one at Conwy (1848) is still in use, but his Britannia Bridge (1850) over the Menai was badly damaged by fire in 1970 and had to be refashioned. It now carries road as well as rail, so reducing the traffic on the suspension bridge.

Also amongst the feats of standard-gauge engineering we can include the line that climbs from Betws-y-coed up the beautiful Lledr valley. It comes up the Conwy from Llandudno Junction to Betws-y-coed as a typical lowland valley line but from Betws onwards becomes decidedly more alpine. Built by the London and North-Western Railway in 1879, this section climbs the narrowing Lledr valley to cross both main road and river on Gethin's Bridge, a monument of Victorian railway grandeur, splendidly ornate and castellated. The name commemorates Owen Gethin Jones of Penmachno, a railway engineer and man of letters. The line goes on to where it can climb no further then plunges through a lordly portal into a 2¼ mile tunnel (the longest in Wales) at the end of which you find yourself deep amongst the slate tips of Blaenau Ffestiniog. Here passengers used to change trains and go on to Bala on the former Great Western line which closed, alas, in 1961. But be not dismayed. For these days you can transfer to the Ffestiniog Railway and have a lovely ride on the narrow-gauge down to Porthmadog.

Entering Snowdonia along the southern border is the celebrated Cambrian Coast line from Shrewsbury which comes down the Dyfi to Machynlleth and crosses the head of the estuary at Dyfi Junction, a station isolated in marshlands with no road to it. The viaduct here is about a hundred and twenty yards long built mostly on wooden piles and partly on steel spans. This line, opened in 1867, goes along the north side of the estuary close to the tidal water, passing through several short tunnels to reach the coast at Aberdyfi where it turns north. The engineering masterpiece on the next stretch is Barmouth Bridge but just before you get there you see the great work of shoring up the sea cliffs to protect the line at Friog where engines have twice met disaster (1883 and 1933) by ploughing into fallen rocks and plunging to the beach, killing driver and fireman on both occasions. A concrete canopy is now built over the line – the only avalanche shelter on a British railway.

The Barmouth viaduct across the Mawddach estuary is nearly half a mile long and consists of 113 spans made of 500 timber piles and two long steel spans, one of which is a swing bridge (still in working order but rarely used) which allows tall-masted ships to enter the estuary. Completed in 1867 the viaduct was substantially rebuilt at the turn of the century. In October 1980 it was closed for extensive repairs when the piles were found to be riddled with timber-eating sea worms. This was a very anxious time for railway devotees who feared that the authorities might use the occasion as an excuse for closing the line (notice of intended closure had been issued in 1971). Bitter political arguments ensued. 'Barmouth Bridge is not just a bridge,' said one commentator, 'it is a debate about rural railways.' In the event the viaduct was repaired, though at vast expense. The most damaged timbers were replaced with greenheart, a tough and durable South American wood known for its worm-resistant properties; and the rest were protected by glass-reinforced cement casings. The line was re-opened in May 1981 amid much rejoicing.

Long stretches of railway belong only to the past but can still be easily traced. There was the one from Bangor to Caernarfon where you could either change for Llanberis or go on to Afon Wen, the junction for Pwllheli and other stations on the Cambrian coast. There was also the delightful line from Barmouth Junction (now Morfa Mawddach) via Dolgellau to Bala, Corwen and Ruabon. It closed in 1964 after a career of ninety-five years. And there was the memorable moorland line, a really momentous journey through the snows of winter, which ran from Blaenau Ffestiniog via Trawsfynydd to Bala. On this line, miles from anywhere, there survives a multi-arched stone viaduct (SH 775388) looking forlorn and incongruous amid the wild uplands. At the south-eastern tip of the Park a short line (closed in 1951) went up the Dyfi valley to link Dinas Mawddwy with the major line at Cemmaes Road. It is sad that most of these old lines were not converted to other public uses. A partial exception is the line from Bala to Barmouth. Alongside Bala Lake it has become a narrow-gauge line, and from Penmaenpool to Barmouth it is now a superb footpath through one of the Park's most delightful regions.

7
BY ROAD, RAIL AND
NARROW-GAUGE

Motorists are very well catered for in Snowdonia. Without ever risking those wriggling, single-track lanes, marked with a T-sign, which die out in the uplands, we can see a huge slice of the Park from the A or B roads. This chapter will deal mainly with the rural scene and the best of the viewpoint roads. For what is of interest in the villages and towns the Gazetteer may be consulted.

The strong northern front of Snowdonia, rising so abruptly near the coast all the way between Conwy and Caernarfon, is best viewed from well outside the Park. From the Great Orme for instance; or Anglesey where perhaps the finest prospect of all is from the shores of Newborough Warren across a fragrant foreground of dunes to a marvellous sweep of all the uplands: Carneddau, Glyder and Snowdon and along the shapely peninsula of Lleyn. On this northern hem of the Park your road from Conwy to Bangor is A55 whose hustling traffic will allow you no time for sight-seeing; but get off it at Penmaenmawr, Llanfairfechan or Abergwyngregyn to enjoy this world of sea and mountain so close beside each other. Alternatively, from Conwy there is the ever-popular Sychnant Pass, a place of rocks, woods, picnic sites and a network of delightful footpaths. Sychnant was the only westward way from Conwy before the modern road was built round the difficult headland of Penmaenbach.

For the exploration of the Conwy valley you have a choice between

A and B roads. A470 will bring you near the National Trust's famous Bodnant garden and on to Llanrwst; or to Capel Garmon and its fine dolmen of Severn-Cotswold type although so far north. Alternatively, you can leave Conwy along B5106 and keep to the west of the river. This road or its tributary lanes will get you to Caerhun Roman fort, the attractive village of Ro-wen, or to Trefriw whence there is a narrow and twisty mountain lane up to Crafnant Lake which has a Forestry Commission car park and woodland trails as well as a path over Mynydd Deulyn to Geirionydd Lake. Crafnant has a lakeside café and from the head of the lake there is a view of the wild woods and crags of Cwm Glas Crafnant national nature reserve.

Returning to Trefriw you can press on south with B5106 to the historic delights of Gwydir Castle (mind you don't run over a peacock) and so to Betws-y-coed. Or at Gwydir you can turn off right to explore a land of old lead mines, new conifer forests and remote lakes like Crafnant and Geirionydd. In places the lane is steep and narrow but there are car parks, picnic spots and trails. Eventually the lane brings you back to A5 at Tŷ Hyll (Ugly House) a mile up the road from Swallow Falls, by far the Park's most visited waterfall. At the Forestry Commission's picnic site between Tŷ Hyll and the falls there are woodland trails and an arboretum.

Of all the Park's major or trunk roads it is A5 that enjoys the most exciting scenery. As you go up to Capel Curig from Betws-y-coed you see a mountain rising ahead in such majesty that newcomers must often mistake it for Snowdon though it is in fact Moel Siabod. Then beyond Capel Curig you go on climbing for another couple of miles until the real mountains begin to show themselves, none more arrestingly than Tryfan which comes to meet you right at the roadside, as forbidding (or inviting) a tower of scree and precipice as you will find anywhere in the Park. There is copious lay-by parking hereabouts where you can pause to enjoy the mountain scene and Ogwen's roadside lake. A5 now slips you between the Glyder range (with Cwm Idwal on your left) and the Carneddau (with the laborious steeps of Pen-yr-ole-wen on your right). Then abruptly you drop down Nant Ffrancon to Bethesda with glimpses on the left of its huge slate quarries, some of which are still working. Just before Bangor you come to the grandiose gates of Penrhyn Castle, one of the National Trust's most visited properties.

At Bangor you have far better reasons for straying out of Snowdonia across the Menai Strait than just to be able to say you have been to the place with the longest name in Britain. Anyway, the name is only a leg-pull and Llanfairpwll (without the rest of it) has a better claim to fame:

Llangelynnin medieval church, three miles south-west of Conwy, stands high on the moorlands near Tal y Fan mountain. The community it once served has long ago dispersed

here in 1915 Britain's first Women's Institute was founded. (The world's first was at Stoney Creek, Ontario, Canada in 1897.) Once you are across the strait, and if you feel you can cope with over a hundred steps, you can climb the Marquess of Anglesey's column which stands at the side of A5 and looks over all this fair Menai region. Plas Newydd, the Marquess's eighteenth-century mansion, is 2 miles south-west along the strait. It now belongs to the National Trust and is open to the public. Its attractions include splendid rooms and furniture, a military museum and paintings by Rex Whistler, including his largest mural. In the spacious grounds is a well-preserved dolmen which, like all such, has long ago lost its original covering mound. But a mile to the west at Bryn Celli Ddu a dolmen in State care has had its mound restored.

From Bangor the attractions of Port Dinorwig, Caernarfon and Llanberis are easily accessible. No one should miss Llanberis Pass which, like Nant Ffrancon, has an A road through it which causes arguments between engineers, who would like to improve the road, and conservationists, who want the road to stay as it is. On the left as you go up are the rocky skirts of Glyder Fawr where climbers can often be seen; and on the right is Cwm Glas-mawr, one of the great corries torn by erosion out of the slopes of Snowdon. Parking is difficult in high summer up the pass and even at the top at Pen-y-pass, despite the large car park; but it is usually available at either end at Nant Peris and by the lake at Pen-y-gwryd. From Pen-y-gwryd it is only a few minutes down the road to Capel Curig and an incomparable prospect of the Snowdon Horseshoe with the Mymbyr lakes in the foreground – surely the most photographed view in all Snowdonia. Another place where the cameras click happily is Nant Gwynant which is soon reached down A498 from Pen-y-gwryd. But pause at the car park viewpoint a mile down the road. It will give you a more intimate look at Snowdon's craggy east face than you will get from any other road.

Nant Gwynant is an Eden of woods, rocks, soaring hillsides and two lovely lakes, the whole perfect scene rounded off by an inspiring view of Moel Hebog ahead of you in the west. Dinas Emrys, a Dark and Middles Ages stronghold, is on your right (SH 606492) and in another mile you reach Beddgelert, gateway to the Pass of Aberglaslyn. There are car parks in Beddgelert and down at Nantmor if you want to go off along the many local footpaths, the most popular of which is the track of the Welsh Highland narrow-gauge railway which used to run down the famous gorge on its way from Dinas Junction (near Caernarfon) to Porthmadog.

At Aberglaslyn Bridge you can chose between A498 and A4085. If you opt for A498 you will carry on down the valley under the densely wooded hem of Moel Ddu, then below the dolerite cliffs of Tremadog national nature reserve and so to Porthmadog. A4085 is narrower and more clambering but it introduces you to the delightful Nantmor country with its woods and wild rocks. Then where the road kinks right to get over the little Croesor stream there is a highly photogenic glimpse of Cnicht rising sharp as a pyramid against the sky. At Garreg you can continue with the A road till it drops between the houses of Penrhyn-deudraeth, crossing the Ffestiniog railway, or you can turn left at Garreg and go meandering along B4410 to Tan-y-bwlch. Just before you get there you see a sign on your left guiding you to Tan-y-bwlch station and your chance of a trip on the narrow-gauge, or a walk through the woods of Coedydd Maentwrog national nature reserve. Or you can carry on down the hill under the iron rail bridge (cast at Boston Lodge, Porthmadog, in 1854) and come to Llyn Mair (Mary's Lake) where you can feed the ducks, coots and gulls. After that it is only a couple of minutes to the Oakeley Arms on A496.

123

Here you are at the entrance to the grounds of Plas Tan-y-bwlch, a mansion built by a former slate quarry owner and now in use as the National Park residential study centre. The village sheltering in the valley below is Maentwrog which is a perfect centre for discovering the many delights of this Vale of Ffestiniog, among them being Rhaeadr Ddu whose waters fall in beauty into a rocky basin amid steep, cool, ferny oakwoods. To get there you can leave your car in a lay–by on A496 a mile south-west of Maentwrog and walk a mile up the wooded glen that comes down from Trawsfynydd reservoir, a glen which narrows higher up into a deep and water-loud gorge called Ceunant Llennyrch.

The Vale has other well-known falls, notably those along the Cynfal stream. For Rhaeadr Cynfal you can leave your car in Ffestiniog village and walk half a mile down through the fields. On the pathside in summer you may see the purple-pink flowers of the upright vetch, a plant formerly common in the Park's more fertile meadows but now getting scarce as the fields are ploughed and reseeded. Down amongst the valley's fine woods of oak and ash, and amid the thunder of water, you descend a flight of steps to a viewing platform where you have the beautiful fall on your left and look straight down into a chasm in which, after rain, the river rages and boils. Ferns in their hundreds adorn the spray-wet rocks; and the tall yellow 'dandelions' among them are in fact marsh hawk's-beards, a real Snowdonian plant little known elsewhere in Wales.

Just up the gorge a tall column of rock stands amidstream, the sort of stack common enough on sea coasts but strange to see in a ravine. It is Huw Llwyd's pulpit, so named for a local mystic who centuries ago is said to have preached or raved from its high top. To get to the other famous falls on this Cynfal stream take B4391 from Ffestiniog for a couple of miles east where you will find a car park on the right (SH 732418). You then walk just up the road to a viewpoint that looks far down to where the waters of Rhaeadr-y-cwm fall and slide most gracefully down a vast, treeless ravine.

You are now getting up to the moorlands ('very wild and barren' George Borrow called them), and the next filling station at Pont yr Afon Gam claims, at 1,255ft (383m), to be the highest in Wales. Ahead of you stretch the squelchy wastes of the Migneint, the Park's biggest area of peat bog, much of it owned by the National Trust. You can pass south of it along B4391 and so to Llyn Celyn and Bala; or you can turn left at Pont yr Afon Gam and take B4407 which twists its way down the moor along with the new-born Conwy river. On your right is first the Migneint then, round the shoulder of a hill, you look back to the great bulge of Arennig Fach and ahead to a high, breezy moorland called Gylchedd. Going down amongst sheltered farmlands and tree-lined lanes you reach the once important village of Ysbyty Ifan, which means Hospice of St John, and come to A5 near Pentrefoelas.

If you now turn left along A5 you will get to Betws-y-coed in 6 miles with the Conwy cascading and splashing among rocks and trees below you all the way. But if you want a round trip back to Ffestiniog you can turn left half-way to Betws-y-coed and follow B4406 up the Machno valley through Penmachno village and under conifered slopes until you are back again high on the moors of Migneint, rejoining B4407 close to a rebuilt but ancient well called Ffynnon Eidda whose inscription *Yf a bydd ddiolchgar* invites you to 'Drink and be thankful'.

For exploring the eastern side of the Park there is no better centre than Bala. Here a favourite day out is to take the Ffestiniog road (A4212) which goes up the Tryweryn valley to Llyn Celyn. The Tryweryn is a powerful little river very popular with canoeists, and just before you get to the reservoir you will find the National White-water Centre where you can see all the excitements, skills and upsets of

On the edge of Llyn Celyn near Bala, in a lay-by on A4212, is this memorial to a Quaker settlement whose site is now drowned. Its persecuted inhabitants emigrated to Pennsylvania in the seventeenth and eighteenth centuries. The mountain beyond is Arennig Fach canoeing down the rapids. Up at the lake there are copious picnic sites with lovely views of Arennig Fawr and Arennig Fach. You can see a lakeside memorial stone to local Quakers who centuries ago emigrated to Pennsylvania to escape persecution. And also by the lake you can visit a modern chapel that remembers Capel Celyn, a Welsh-speaking hamlet that was drowned to create this reservoir which supplies Liverpool with water and also prevents flooding down the Dee. The building of the reservoir (1965) remains a source of bitter resentment amongst Welsh patriots.

For far views of the Park's eastern frontier you can turn left on your way back to Bala and make for Cerrigydrudion along B4501. For several miles this road is the boundary of the Park and in summer you will see miles of the hedgerows showing the pale flower-spikes of the willow-leaved spiraea (see p 55). At Nantycwrtiau telephone kiosk the Park boundary and a narrow lane both fork left to climb steadily for the open moors until you reach the hill top called Cadair Benllyn and can look across to cairn-topped Carnedd y Filiast – the highest point in this corner of the Park. At Cadair Benllyn you may well prefer to turn back rather than risk the tortuous, narrow lanes that lie ahead between you and A5.

South of Bala the extreme south-east corner of the Park, around the village of Rhos-y-gwaliau, is much afflicted by the conifers of Penllyn (or Aberhirnant) Forest but there is still some high ground rising clear above the spruce blanket. Within the forest there are walks and picnic places. Outside it you can drive round the Park boundary along the Welshpool road (B4391) to the Berwyn moorland watershed at Milltir Gerrig, beyond which you are out of the Park. Or, starting from Rhos-y-gwaliau, you can drive through the forest up the minor road that goes over and down to Lake Vyrnwy, but you will not escape from the trees until you come near to the head of Cwm Hirnant and have Foel y Geifr just across the moor on your right.

If you want a good walk into the heart of the region you can set out from the lakeside car park at Llangywair (Llangower) along the leafy lane up Glyn Gywair and find your way from there to the top of Foel y Geifr. From Llangywair you can go on almost into Llanuwchllyn and turn left up a road which climbs to the pass of Bwlch-y-groes where the car park looks north to Arennig across a great reach of country. From here you can go on down to Lake Vyrnwy where birdwatchers can visit the RSPB reserve (information centre near the dam) and see goosanders and other waterfowl as well as plenty of woodland birds. The alternative route from Bwlch-y-groes – a real scenic spectacular – is to go down

126

into the Dyfi valley and so to A470 at Dinas Mawddwy. Note however that all these Bwlch-y-groes roads are single tracks with few passing places and cannot be recommended to motorists with no love of steep drops below them.

Another road with little in its favour for those who dislike mountain lanes full of tight squeezes is the one over the moors from Llanuwchllyn to Trawsfynydd. But no doubt others will enjoy its loneliness and its unique views of Moel Llyfnant and neighbouring hills. The much faster and smoother alternative to this upland adventure is A494 which soon gets you to Dolgellau down the wide Wnion valley with the whole range of Cader Idris building up before you. From Dolgellau you can turn north for Trawsfynydd up A470, the first village you reach being Llanelltyd which has an interesting old church and is near the meagre ruins of Cymer Abbey. At the second village, Ganllwyd, there is the National Trust estate of Dolmelynllyn (see p 80). North of Ganllwyd you enter the conifers of Coed y Brenin where there are picnic sites and a choice of well-marked trails. There is an interesting arboretum a mile west of Llanfachreth; and at the Maesgwm visitor centre 2 miles north of Ganllwyd you can learn about forestry, wildlife, gold mines, drovers' roads and other local matters.

West from Dolgellau goes A496 for ten winding miles to the sea at Barmouth. Great slopes of rock and wood – the southernmost skirts of Rhinog – soar upwards on your right while on your left you have wide views of Cader Idris across the Mawddach. Along the south side of the estuary runs a parallel road (A493) which looks to the hills in the north where they build up to the top of Diffwys. At Penmaenpool toll-bridge there is an interpretive centre providing information about local natural history. Here too is the start of the footpath which goes along the old railway to the coast.

The main road south from Dolgellau (A470) climbs towards the east end of Cader Idris by way of the Cross Foxes Inn. Here the road divides. A470 continues up over the bleak Oerddrws Pass and down a spectacular valley to Dinas Mawddwy and Mallwyd. Or you can turn right at Cross Foxes along A487 with a view ahead into the great corrie of Cwm Geu Graig on Cader Idris. Then you go down the magnificent pass under the cliffs of Craig y Llam with Talyllyn Lake spread across the valley floor ahead. Turning off right at the bottom of the pass you can take B4405 along the edge of the lake where in summer you may see great crested grebes and in winter many ducks and coots. Next village down the valley is Abergynolwyn where some car passengers take a ride on the Talyllyn Railway to be met at the other end at Tywyn. But for a car the most scenic route is reached by turning right at Abergynolwyn along the lane which follows the Dysynni river, passing near the medieval Castell y Bere and under the crags and screes of Bird Rock, home of many cormorants and other birds.

The southern edge of the Park is marked by the Dyfi river at Machynlleth and from there to the coast by its estuary. From Machynlleth it is 3 miles north up A487 to the Centre for Alternative Technology which occupies an old slate quarry and is visible from afar as a place of windmills. Further up the road on the left is a Forestry Commission picnic site (with woodland trail) and then you come to the former slate-quarrying village of Corris where there are gift and craft shops along the main road. All up the valley from Machynlleth you will have the course of the old narrow-gauge slate railway close on your right; and at Aberllefenni you will find slate still being worked, though only on a small scale, and see a mountain which has been quite hollowed out by quarrying.

The 10 miles from Machynlleth to Aberdyfi are beautiful all the way. The only village is Pennal which looks north to the long, high, smooth ridge of Tarren Hendre and sister heights. Then 2 miles west of Pennal the road rises to give far southward views across the wide estuary to the foothills of Plynlimon. A more sequestered route to the coast turns right at the hamlet of Cwrt, half a mile west of Pennal, and follows a narrow, climbing road that brings you to Cwm Maethlon (Happy Valley). There is a car park here on the left (SN 641987), starting point for the 1 mile walk up to Llyn Barfog (the Bearded Lake) and the echoing rock beyond. For a seaboard run from Aberdyfi or Tywyn take A493 which goes inland to Bryncrug, crosses the Dysynni river near an ancient bridge and curves back to the coast to become a high-level, far-seeing road that in places is right above the shore. Along this seaside route you come to the primitive cliff-top church of Llangelynnin (SH 571071) and then the popular holiday villages of Llwyngwril and Fairbourne.

Standard-gauge railways

In our historical look at the Park's railways (Chapter 6) we saw that, despite heavy losses, Snowdonia is still connected with the outside world on three sides. Along the north coast the London–Holyhead line serves Conwy, Penmaenmawr, Llanfairfechan and Bangor. In the south and west there is the line from Shrewsbury to Dyfi Junction which then becomes the Cambrian Coast line to Pwllheli calling at many small stations which can be used for exploring nearby parts of the Park.

For a rail tour right across as well as round the Park you can go from Bangor to Llandudno Junction, changing there for the Conwy valley line up to Blaenau Ffestiniog. From there you go down the vale on the narrow-gauge, transferring back to the standard-gauge at Minffordd and so down the coast to Machynlleth or Aberystwyth.

Narrow-gauge lines

The Talyllyn

Ever since 1866 and even through two world wars this delightful little line (27in gauge) has been carrying people between Tywyn on the coast of Cardigan Bay and the former slate-quarrying village of Abergynolwyn (in the parish of Talyllyn) 7 miles inland. So it claims a record as the longest (in time), continually operating, narrow-gauge steam passenger railway in the world. Its main original purpose was, however, the conveyance of slates from a quarry up in the hills south of Abergynolwyn, the slates coming down to railway level by way of steep inclines. When quarrying ceased in 1946 the line would certainly have closed had it not been for the personal devotion of its proprietor, Sir Henry Haydon Jones, who kept it going, no doubt at a loss, until he died in 1950. That really did look like the end of the line but again it was saved, this time by the intervention of a society of amateur rail enthusiasts.

The Talyllyn Railway Preservation Society was born at a meeting in Birmingham in 1950 and by an immense labour of love has managed to convert what had become a very run-down railway into the thriving enterprise it is today, giving pleasure to thousands of holiday-makers as well as joy to rail enthusiasts world-wide. In 1976 it even extended the line for nearly another mile into the difficult river gorge of Nant Gwernol at the foot of what used to be the slate quarry incline. The old rails and sleepers have all been replaced, the rolling stock carefully maintained and increased, and new stations have been built in traditional style. The terminus at Tywyn has been redesigned to include a museum full of nostalgia not only for the early days of this railway but for old narrow-gauge lines elsewhere, including America.

The line's oldest engines are *Talyllyn* (0–4–2) built at Whitehaven, Cumberland in 1864, and *Dolgoch* (0–4–0) built there in 1866. To these the Preservation Society was able to add two locomotives from the defunct Corris Railway in 1951, the older of which was built at Loughborough in 1878. The total number of steam engines is now six. The stock of carriages, three of which date back to the earliest days, has likewise been added to.

A train on the Talyllyn narrow-gauge railway climbs through an oakwood above Dolgoch. Since 1950 the survival of this old line has been entirely due to the Talyllyn Railway Preservation Society

The journey along this much-cherished mini-railway (about two hours there and back) is altogether beautiful and totally unsmirched by the quarries, for they are in the uplands well out of sight. The line climbs very gently along the side of a deep, wide valley green with pastures and trees, gradually bringing you up into stronger country as Cader Idris appears in the north and the foothills of Tarren Hendre get ever steeper in the south. Geographically the valley is something of a mystery. It must have been cut by a river but although at first there is the little Pathew brook, you discover as you get higher that there is no stream at all, just a broad, U-shaped, dry valley. So what has happened?

To find out more you need to go to Abergynolwyn. There you can hardly avoid guessing that the Dysynni river which comes hastening down from Talyllyn Lake must once have flowed straight on down what is now the Pathew valley, for that still looks the natural way for it to go – following the broad, straight trench that is part of the Bala-Tywyn fault-line. So why and when did the Dysynni jink sideways at Abergynolwyn and go twisting into the next valley north where it has flowed ever since, taking the Nant Gwernol tributary with it? Was it a simple case of river capture, the result of freak work by glaciers or some other cause? It is a matter about which geographers continue to debate.

The various stations along the line are starting points for either gentle strolls or serious mountain walks. From Rhyd-yr-onnen there is an easy safari of 4 miles through a gap in the hills to Pant-yr-on near the head of Cwm Maethlon (Happy Valley). From there you can go on east to Cwrt and Pennal or return into the west to Aberdyfi or Tywyn. Scenically the most attractive station is Dolgoch, not only for its viaduct high over a gorge but also for the steep oakwoods that surround it and all the lovely walks through the trees to nearby cascades and waterfalls. Above the highest fall of this hanging valley you are soon clear of the woods and heading for the long, undulating ridge which, so tradition tells us, was on the line of Ffordd Cadfan, a medieval pilgrims' way from England across Wales to Tywyn and over the sea to the holy island of Bardsey. Today no pilgrims come that way except those with a fervour for gaining the tops of Tarren-y-gesail, Tarren Hendre and the other far-seeing heights.

Walks in many directions radiate from the line's two highest stations – Abergynolwyn and Nant Gwernol. You can climb the steep southward lane to the remains of the Bryneglwys quarries which year by year are vanishing among the conifers. Road undreamt of by the quarrymen now go far through the forests, and from the station at Nant Gwernol there are forest walks especially designed for those who come up on the trains. You can also walk down to Abergynolwyn village and its slate museum, or go up the Dysynni to Talyllyn Lake or downstream to the ruins of Castell y Bere. For a more ambitious excursion you can go to Llanfihangel-y-pennant and climb Cader Idris from the west.

If you are curious about that sideways jerk the Dysynni makes in its course at Abergynolwyn you may like to explore the mile or so of sinuous gorge it has carved north-west out of the village. You cross the Gwernol stream and follow the footpath along the left bank of the

Dysynni under the slopes of Gamallt. Below you the river splashes
through its rocks from pool to pool where patient anglers dream of great
sea trout and even vaster salmon. The path ends at Pont Ystumanner,
a name of much history hereabouts, for in the days of commotes and
hundreds (and who knows how much further back?) Ystumanner was
the name of all this district. At the bridge you can return to Abergynolwyn along a lane high up on the other side of the valley, perhaps getting
a new angle on the problem of why the river changed its course.

The Ffestiniog
'One of the wonders of Wales' was the verdict on this railway by *Jenkin-
son's Practical Guide to North Wales* in 1878.

> Being the first example of the narrow-gauge lines running upwards
> amongst the mountains, it may stand in the same category as the lines
> at the collieries near Newcastle which were the earliest locomotive rail-
> ways in England. Leaving the Cambrian train at Minffordd Junction,
> the traveller walks up a path to the toy line and enters one of the little
> carriages; and though on so small a gauge, they are as comfortable as
> those on other lines. Some of the engines are of peculiar construction
> and are known as Fairlie's 'double bogie' patent. The train gradually
> ascends and winds on very sharp curves round the sides of the Moelwyn
> mountain range, sometimes passing through thick woods and a few
> tunnels with the verdant vale deep below . . .. The line ends at Diffwys
> station at Blaenau Ffestiniog in the midst of houses and the bustle con-
> nected with slate works.

Thanks entirely to the dedication of narrow-gauge devotees this historic
line still exists in perfect health and is open to tourist traffic much as it
was last century except that most passengers now get on at Porthmadog.

In was in 1836 that the rails of what was to become one of the world's
most famous narrow-gauge railways were laid down on a line so skilfully
gradiented that waggons carrying slate could roll down it gently by
gravity for its whole 14 miles. Horses, which had been carried down
with the slate trams, then hauled the empty trucks back up to Blaen-
nau. It may sound laborious but it was a vast improvement on the previous system under which the slate was carried from the quarries to the
nearest roads in panniers on ponies' backs, then by horse and cart to
the estuary, then by barge to the coast.

The horse-drawn railway worked for nearly three decades until in
1863 came the revolution: in defiance of the country's top-flight
engineers, who declared that steam haulage was suitable only for stan-

132

A down-train at Tan-y-bwlch station on the Ffestiniog narrow-gauge railway.
After years of neglect the line was re-opened along its entire length in 1982 and
is immensely popular

dard-gauge use, the Ffestiniog line (1ft 11½in) went over to steam
when two engines, *The Princess* (made in London) and *Mountaineer*
(made in New Jersey, USA) were brought by rail to Caernarfon, then
by horse and cart to Porthmadog. Next year two more locomotives
arrived and were named *The Prince* and *Palmerston*. Of these four, two
have survived though very little of their original fabric can now remain.
The Prince is still working and *The Princess* is at present taking a rest in

the museum at Porthmadog narrow-gauge station. She has the distinction of being the first locomotive in the world to work on a public narrow-gauge railway.

After two years of hauling slate waggons the railway began a passenger service on 6 January 1865, the first narrow-gauge to do so in Great Britain. It proved so popular that more engines were acquired, notably the extra-powerful double-bogie Fairlie articulated locos, machines of strange appearance that look like two engines welded together back to back. The first, made by G. England and Co, London, arrived in 1869. It aroused international interest and representatives came from Russia, India and other countries interested in building railways in regions too mountainous for standard-gauge lines. Eventually two Fairlies were even built by the Ffestiniog Railway itself in its works at Boston Lodge which is at the other end of the Cob (embankment) from Porthmadog. These new locos were *Merddin Emrys* (1879), which is still working, and *Livingstone Thompson* (1886), which is at present in storage. Boston Lodge is named after Boston in Lincolnshire, a memory of the fact that William Alexander Madocks (1773–1828) who completed the Cob in 1811, was MP for Boston.

Towards the end of the century the fortunes of the little railway declined, much of the slate-carrying trade having been taken from it by the London and North-Western Railway, which came up the Conwy valley to Blaenau Ffestiniog in 1879, and by the Great Western, which got there from Bala in 1883. But the arrival of these giants was not all loss: tourism increased greatly as the fashion grew of transferring from narrow-gauge to standard-gauge at Blaenau for visits to Betws-y-coed and stations north. Difficulties, however, went on increasing in the twentieth century as the slate industry went into recession and all railways felt ever more challenged by road traffic. The narrow-gauge kept going through two world wars but closed in 1946, leaving the whole system of rails and rolling stock to fall victim to decay and vandalism for the next eight years.

In 1954, encouraged by what was being done on the Talyllyn line, volunteers converged on Porthmadog and began to restore the Ffestiniog (for tradition's sake it is often, though less correctly, spelt with one F as it was in the beginning). It was an exciting moment when the first train crossed the Cob with passengers in August 1955. Minffordd was reached a year later, Penrhyn the year after that and by 1958 trains were getting to Tan-y-bwlch, over 7 miles from Porthmadog. In that year 60,000 passengers were carried. Ten years passed before the next station, Dduallt, was opened. Then came the *pièce de résistance*: to avoid the new hydro-electricity reservoir at Tanygrisiau, which has flooded the old line, the narrow-gauge was rerouted to turn a complete circle and cross over itself, so getting far enough up the hillside to be able to pass well above the reservoir. But before it could do that a long new tunnel had to be blasted through hard rocks. On 25 May 1982 came the day of triumph when the line became officially open all the way to Blaenau Ffestiniog, the little trains coming in alongside the standard-gauge, so making the transfer of passengers to the Conwy valley line a very easy matter.

This link with the Conwy valley is only one of the many attractions of the Ffestiniog line. The Vale itself, though so celebrated, was never easy to get to until the railway came. Then suddenly the woods, water-falls and mountains were within everyone's reach. And still today Tan-y-bwlch station is a favourite starting point for Rhaeadr Ddu falls, the Coedydd Maentwrog nature trails or climbing Moelwyn Bach whose rugged peak rises so close in the north. The station at Tanygrisiau also gives access to the Moelwyn range as well as to the power-station and its excellent visitor centre. And up at Blaenau Ffestiniog there are the slate quarries to visit and many walks on the hills above.

The Welsh Highland

A close neighbour of the Ffestiniog line and likewise promoted by a dedicated restoration society is the Welsh Highland Railway. It begins close to Porthmadog's British Rail station but as yet it goes only to a temporary terminus, and you're there and back in half an hour. It was opened by the society in August 1980 and when legal difficulties have been overcome the intention is to rebuild as much as possible of the original line which ran for 21 miles to Caernarfon and was the longest narrow-gauge in Wales. Its life was short and difficult. Incorporating sections of much older lines, it opened in 1922 but failed to compete with the ever-increasing road traffic and was closed in 1937. The restored line, though so brief, is well equipped with locos and coaches and its sponsors have great faith in its future.

The Corris

In the Park's deep south another hopeful society has ambitions to restore the narrow-gauge line (2ft 3in) which used to link the slate quarries up at Aberllefenni and Corris with the standard-gauge line down in the Dyfi valley at Machynlleth. During its career the Corris steam railway carried both goods and passengers. It was closed in 1948 but you can see two of its engines, now named *Sir Haydn* and *Edward*

135

Thomas, still working on the Talyllyn Railway. Restoration of the Corris line is in its earliest stages and no trains are yet running. You will find a short length of track at Corris, where there is also a small railway museum. For the Park's other narrow-gauge enterprises see the Gazetteer under Bala Lake, Fairbourne, Llanberis and Snowdon Mountain Railway.

8
EXPLORING ON FOOT

Snowdonia abounds with footpaths. Some, like those up Snowdon, are used by the whole world and need Herculean labours to maintain them. Others in less popular areas are so little frequented that they can be quite hard to find though they may begin with a very promising stile and a Llwybr Cyhoeddus/Public Footpath notice. A few trails go far across country; many are strolls of less than an hour. This chapter can hope to indicate only a few of the more important pathways, mostly on the uplands; the rest can easily be found on maps, especially the OS 1:25000 Outdoor Leisure Maps.

Snowdon

There are six well-known trails up Snowdon (3,560ft/1,085m). In the north is the Llanberis path which, not straying far from the mountain railway, is the longest (5 miles) but least severe. Perhaps, as is often asserted, it is also the dullest, especially the lower half. But nearer the top you get some superb glimpses down into Llanberis Pass and there is no better view of the huge cliffs of Clogwyn Du'r Arddu and their sharply downfolded strata.

Two Snowdon trails, the Pig Track and the Miners' Track, (both about 3½ miles) start from the east at Pen-y-pass and eventually merge. The Pig Track goes boldly up through the rocks as if its goal were Crib Goch, which from this angle is everyone's idea of a mountain peak and is often mistaken for Snowdon itself. But the Pig Track does not tackle Crib Goch. Instead it slips across the south face, climbing steadily at first, then by steep zigzags, to reach the col between Crib-y-ddysgl and Snowdon, so joining the Llanberis path to the summit. These days its name is often spelt 'Pyg Track' in the belief that it began as 'P-y-g' and is short for Pen-y-gwyrd. But before 'Pyg' was invented early this century, the guidebooks used to know this route as 'the Pig Track' and this is no doubt the correct version. It is probably so called because it goes through a gap called Bwlch Moch ('the pass of the pigs'), a perhaps very ancient name. Another possible explanation of 'Pig Track' is that it is really the 'peak track', *pig* being Welsh for peak.

The Miners' Track sets out on a comparatively genteel course past Llyn Teyrn and the ruins of the miners' barracks. It then crosses Llyn Llydaw on a causeway, passes the copper ore-crushing sheds and makes more steeply for Llyn Glaslyn with very photogenic views of Snowdon round many a bend. Above Llyn Glaslyn you face a serious scramble past the old mine and up to the Pig Track. But if you feel breathless on the way remember the chaps who used to hump sacks of ore up that same route. This approach to Snowdon, by Pig Track or Miners' Track, is certainly the most spectacular. No other flank of the mountain has broken up into quite such extensive precipices as those of Lliwedd which drop straight down to Llyn Llydaw and those of Snowdon's east face, Clogwyn y Garnedd, hanging high above Llyn Glaslyn.

Another popular route climbs from the south up Cwm y Llan. Starting from Nant Gwynant you follow an old slate quarry road past the Gladstone Rock where in 1892 the eighty-four-year-old prime minister officially opened the new path created by his friend Sir Edward Watkin who owned that side of the mountain. (Ten years earlier, Watkin had begun work on the Channel Tunnel at Dover, only to be stopped by the government.) The Watkin Path gets very steep near the summit and can be truly hazardous in ice and snow.

The two trails on the western side of Snowdon (about 3½ miles) both set off from the Caernarfon–Beddgelert road. One begins at the village of Rhyd-ddu and is soon joined by a path that comes up from Beddgelert by way of Pitt's Head, a rock on the side of A4085 2 miles north-west of Beddgelert. The other track starts from the banks of Llyn Cwellyn near the Snowdon Ranger youth hostel. This western side of Snowdon gives you magnificent views of the Nantlle hills and the Hebog group but for much of the way the paths are on moorland rather than mountain and so have fewer devotees than Snowdon's other trails. But traditionalists prefer to go up from Snowdon Ranger because that was the route most favoured by the earliest tourists.

Whichever way they get to the summit, most walkers seem to take about three hours up and two down. This allows time for taking many a breather, admiring the view or eating a sandwich. The summit café is open whenever the railway is running, that is on most days in the summer. But Snowdon is much climbed even in midwinter: and when frozen or snowy, the slopes and rocks can be extremely treacherous. Accidents are not uncommon at any season and are often the result of slipping off innocent-looking footpaths above steep slopes. There is every need to go properly equipped and to exercise extreme care. Even in summer dry grassy slopes can be dangerously slippery.

The Snowdon Horseshoe

Nowhere is care needed more than on this high-level circular route (about 7 miles) which includes the summit of Snowdon and is one of the finest ridge walks in Europe. It is usually tackled anticlockwise from Pen-y-pass. You set off along the Pig Track then work your way up the rocks to the bare, knife-edge formed by the ancient lavas of Crib Goch. This is a really choice exercise in scrambling, with an abyss below you on both sides. Then, having negotiated (or sidled round) some awkward towers called the Pinnacles, you descend to a col called Bwlch Coch before rising again to Crib-y-ddysgl (which is also called Garnedd Ugain). There is another dip where the Pig Track comes up from the left and in ten minutes you are on Snowdon summit.

Now begins the easier half of the Horseshoe. A descent and a climb bring you to the second knife-edge, this time that of Lliwedd. Then comes the long final arm of the Horseshoe, descending and curving round and back to Pen-y-pass. This is an all-day expedition for most of us and not to be contemplated, especially in winter, unless you are really fit, accustomed to mountains, properly clothed and equipped and have a head for heights. Athletes have run it with incredible speed. It has even been walked no-handed with snow on the ground.

The Glyder range

Pen-y-pass opens the gate not only to Snowdon but also, in the opposite direction, to the beckoning heights of Glyder which, along with Cader Idris far away in the south, is the Park's most popular upland after the Snowdon group. A path to Glyder leaves Pen-y-pass at the side of the youth hostel, but before you go racing for the summit you might like to consider the more gentle stroll up Moel Berfedd, the hill between Pen-y-pass and Pen-y-gwryd. This modest peak enjoys a wonderful view of Snowdon peeping over the shoulder of Crib Goch and was the vantage point chosen by the Romantic artist S. R. Percy (1821–86) for his well-known painting of Snowdon.

The Glyder range, neatly defined by the deep valleys that surround it, is climbed from many points. A traditional route in the south comes up from Pen-y-gwryd, slips between Glyder Fach and Tryfan and so down the magnificent Cwm Bochlwyd to Ogwen. It is a mere 3 miles when drawn straight across the map but is a plod of several hours for the average hill walker. This path is part of a 12 mile trek the copper miners used to make weekly between their homes in Bethesda and the Glaslyn mine on Snowdon. Imagine crossing Glyder to get to and from work in midwinter!

The long narrow Glyder range everywhere stands high and all ways to it are steep. From its sharp eastern angle at Capel Curig it can be tackled lengthwise on an exhilarating 6-mile route that looks down one superb corrie after another all the way to Glyder Fawr (3,279ft/999m). From there you can descend via the Devil's Kitchen to Ogwen. Or if you have enough puff you can loop in Y Garn as well and come down by way of Cwm Clyd. All along the tops you will find a wilderness of stones and woolly-haired moss beneath your feet. And here and there, especially on Glyder Fach (3,262ft/994m), you will see strange piles of mountain-top wreckage standing about the landscape like the remains of some lost civilisation, which is what earlier explorers thought they were. It was an understandable error because many of these great slabs – the result of jointing – are as smooth and square as if shaped by human hands.

Neighbour to Glyder Fach on the north-east is the ever-popular Tryfan (3,010ft/917m) up which three routes from Llyn Ogwen are particularly favoured. One starts from the western end of the lake along the Cwm Idwal trail but soon branches left and goes up past Llyn Bochlwyd, making for the gap between Tryfan and Glyder Fach, the track along which the miners used to plod their way to Snowdon. Well before you reach the watershed you turn left along a path that has been well marked out by the thousands who have gone before you. It is a steep pull up to the summit and its two massive pillars, Adam and Eve. They may look as if they have been deliberately set up like standing stones but in fact they are the natural products of mountain-top decay. The more agile among us clamber up them and leap nonchalantly from one to the other.

The pile of slates on the top of Glyder Fach is the result of jointing and erosion. The rock is rhyolite, an acid lava which also forms the cliffs of nearby Tryfan and the Idwal Slabs so well-known to climbers

It is from the east end of Ogwen Lake that the other two paths set out. One makes without compromise for the formidable northern ridge from near a favourite climbers' playground called the Milestone Buttress and is the hardest way to the top. The other goes slanting up the Heather Terrace, a conspicuous feature of the east face. It climbs up the bedding plane of the rocks below more cliffs which have long been a climbers' paradise. But whichever way you tackle Tryfan you can expect a real scramble. And be prepared to look down awesome drops. For Tryfan is the Glyder group's answer to Crib Goch.

The northern third of the Glyderau, to give the range its plural name, is less frequented because although its summits are fine viewpoints they do not have quite the mountainy qualities of those above Cwm Idwal. But the north has one great attraction in Elidir Fawr (3,030ft/924m) which acts like a magnet for that numerous group who aspire to conquer all Snowdonia's 3,000-footers. Elidir Fawr can be climbed from various directions. If you go up from Ogwen you start at a thousand feet (300m) but face a hard initial climb out of Cwm Idwal before you turn north to take in Y Garn (3,104ft/946m) on the way.

141

The path from Nant Peris begins at less than 400ft (120m) and the going up the Dudodyn valley is rather a plod; but things improve when you get to the corrie cliffs above Llyn Marchlyn Mawr with its great prospects of Anglesey in the north and Snowdon in the south.

From Elidir Fawr the rest of the neighbouring summits are within easy reach: Carnedd y Filiast (2,695ft/821m), Mynydd Perfedd (2,665ft/812m) and Foel Goch (2,727ft/831m). Alternatively, they can be tackled from Nant Ffrancon up Cwm Bual starting at Ty-gwyn; or from outside the Park in the north from Bethesda, Bryn Eglwys and other points. For those with no mountaineering ambitions who simply want to enjoy the quiet beauty of Nant Ffrancon there is the old road from Ogwen down the west side of the vale for 3 miles, rejoining A5 at Ty'n-y-maes. Before you start down this road have a peep under the main road bridge (Pont Pen-y-benglog) at the remains of the eighteenth-century bridge fossilised beneath it.

The Carneddau

These lofty moorlands, forming Snowdonia's widest plateau, rise to peaks which, after Snowdon's twin summits (Yr Wyddfa and Crib-y-ddysgl), are the highest in England and Wales. On all sides they present a stern face to the world but once you have made it up those first forbidding slopes you have miles of easier uplands before you with glimpses down long deep valleys or vast corries, some with precipices plunging far down to deep cold lakes. The south-western half of the Carneddau is most commonly approached from the A5 near Ogwen, the first peak to be won being Pen-yr-ole-wen which, at 3,210ft (979m), is much the same height as England's highest mountain, Scafell Pike.

Unless you are really looking for trouble you will not throw yourself into a direct confrontation with Pen-yr-ole-wen from the western end of Ogwen Lake. Go instead to the other end of the lake and make your way more gently up from Tal y Llyn Ogwen farm to Llyn Ffynnon Lloer, a small tarn hidden from the world below and beautifully half-circled around by dark crags and pale screes, a quiet cwm and perhaps it always has been: for there seems little trace of early or recent habitation, no scar of mine or quarry. On Pen-yr-ole-wen's flat top, whose views are across all the Glyderau, you may notice that not all the little round leaves under your feet are those of bilberry: many belong to the dwarf willow which here is very dwarf indeed because of all the trampling it receives. Yet miraculously it survives and even flowers.

From Pen-yr-ole-wen you turn north-east up an easy slope of bare scree to the top of Carnedd Dafydd (3,426ft/1,044m) which is a dome of shattered rocks with hardly a green blade in sight. The path now drops to the col between Dafydd and Llywelyn and you find yourself looking straight down the precipices of Ysgolion Duon (the Black Ladders) which you will see are not darkly mantled with heather but are green with many different plants – a sign that the dolerite here yields enough calcium for lime-loving plants. Indeed, this great corrie that faces down to Bethesda has long been a happy hunting ground for botanists.

Llywelyn's top (3,484ft/1,062m), the highest of the Carneddau, is even more of a rock desert than Dafydd's and where it falls away towards neighbouring Yr Elen (3,152ft/961m) there are groups of upstanding rock slabs reminiscent of those on Glyder Fach. From Llywelyn a well-trodden track goes down and quickly up again to Yr Elen which from here looks like a mountain sliced in half, so precipitous is its eastern side. From that sharp ridge you can either go on down to Bethesda (3½ miles) or return to Llywelyn and carry on northwards across the Carneddau, taking in Foel Grach (3,196ft/974m) and Foel Fras (3,092ft/942m), so accomplishing one of the major ridge walks of Wales. Then you can take one of several ways down to the coast road between Abergwyngregyn and Conwy. But for those seeking a different way back from Llywelyn to Ogwen there is the popular 5-mile descent by way of Pen y Waun Wen (the top of the much-climbed Craig yr Ysfa) and then down past Ffynnon Llugwy reservoir.

Those who walk up the Carneddau from the north coast are the bravest of all because they start right down at sea level. But without being so ambitious you can still enjoy these long seaward slopes, for there are many walks that will not occupy all of a summer's day. You can follow the many paths up from Llanfairfechan or Penmaenmawr. Or there are the walks which start from the Sychnant Pass going either north to Conwy Mountain or south to Bwlch y Ddeufaen. Or you can contour round the slopes of the stony hill called Moel Lus along the Jubilee Trail, enjoying views in every direction. The top of Moel Lus will give you even wider prospects.

The Carneddau uplands may be tight and strong in the west above Nant Ffrancon but in the east they are penetrated by long valleys cut by streams that find their swift way down to the lower Conwy. Up these valleys go narrow, winding lanes which falter then die where they reach the moorland but then they become footpaths to lead you to the summits. The most historic of these routes we have met already, the one through the gap of Bwlch y Ddeufaen in the north, starting from Ro-wen. South of this is the path which goes steadfastly west-south-west across country from above Llanbedr-y-cennin to cross the summit ridge a little south of Foel Fras, descending to the lowlands north of Bethesda, making a total walk of a dozen or so splendid miles.

The south-western part of the Carneddau region is Snowdonia's lakeland. All these waters are accessible by footpath and a few by metalled roads. From Talybont a long lane climbs 4 miles south-west to peter out on the moors east of Llyn Eigiau. Footpaths off it lead you to a pair of lakes, Dulyn and Melynllyn, which lie deep and cold under corrie cliffs. Or you can swing south past Eigiau's shattered dam and up the great cwm beyond, with shapely Llithrig-y-wrach above you on your left. The valley curves right round to the north, getting rockier and wilder all the way. If it is spring or early summer you will hear the piping of ring ouzels and the chack-chacking of anxious wheatears amongst the block scree, and perhaps the songs of sandpipers along the lake's inlet stream. You pass extensive slate quarry ruins and tips and then the cliffs of Craig yr Ysfa are above you. A stiffish clamber takes you up to Carnedd Llywelyn, passing a rather strange flat stony plateau (a glacial effect) called Gledrffordd.

Llyn Geirionydd on the east side of the Carneddau, three miles north-west of Betws-y-coed, is a popular lake for water sports

South again are other inviting paths and lanes that go up from Dol-garrog and Trefriw over the hills south-west to Capel Curig. One of them skirts Llyn Cowlyd, formerly a deep natural lake, now an even deeper reservoir. It is the longest lake in the Park after those at Trawsfynydd and Bala. The path keeps to the northern edge of the water and looks across to the towering, dark, plant-rich cliffs of Creigiau Gleision. At the south-western end of the lake the path slips you through a gap and you are soon down to A5 near Capel Curig, the total distance being about 8 miles. The country south-east of Llyn Cowlyd is mostly within the empire of the Forestry Commission and the paths available are many. A favourite circular walk goes from A5 near Capel Curig youth hostel over the hills to Llyn Crafnant, then it climbs round the north end of Mynydd Deulyn and returns down the western shore of Llyn Geirionydd and back over the top to Crafnant. From there you retrace your steps to Capel Curig. Information about other walks and forest trails in this area is available at the Park visitor centre in Betws-y-coed.

Mynydd Mawr to Moel Hebog

Mynydd Mawr (2,290ft/698m) is the very bulky hill that looks at Snowdon from across Llyn Cwellyn. It is similarly isolated from its neighbours to the south by the deep east-west trench of the Nantlle valley. There are routes coming up from the west to Mynydd Mawr but it is most often climbed from Rhyd-ddu by a 3-mile path that takes you gently up through the conifers above the lake. You are then faced with an awkward grassy slope before it eases off above the profoundly gullied cliffs of Craig y Bera which stare into the midday sun. From there you swing north to the rounded summit which, like so many, is a bare expanse of small stones. The views are not only of Snowdon in the east but also of the Menai Strait and Anglesey in the north. Far in the south-west rises Yr Eifl and close in the south are all those friendly-looking heights clustered south of the Nantlle valley.

For this compact group the village of Rhyd-ddu is a favourite starting point. The nearest of them is Y Garn (2,080ft/634m) and if you feel strong enough you can make a frontal attack on it but many prefer to take it from the rear by setting off south-west through the forestry to the pass of Bwlch-y-ddwy-elor. From there you skirt northwards round the top of the plantations to the twin summits of Trum y Ddysgl (2,329ft/710m) and Mynydd Drws-y-coed which look down a fine corrie whose cliffs are well clothed with mountain plants. You can now follow the

145

crags north to Y Garn; or you can turn west and after an easy descent and rise you come up to Mynydd Tal-y-mignedd (2,148ft/655m) which is identified by a tall tower, presumably a folly, which has been there since at least 1869, as a local estate map shows.

The hills go splendidly on into the south-west, all linked by a well-trodden path. But you need to be in good heart for the next height, Craig Cwm Silyn – at 2,408ft/734m it is the highest of this group – because you must first scramble a long way down into the Pass of Bwlch Dros-bern and immediately climb just as steeply up. From Craig Cwm Silyn you can follow the line of craggy tops that look down to a corrie lake far below and across all the Nantlle slate region. Then, still going south-west, you once more lose height but soon rise yet again, this time to the wild rocks of Carnedd-goch (2,298ft/700m). You now go due south, keeping up out of Cwm Dulyn on your right and Cwm Ciprwth on your left, before you turn into the west and reach yet another rocky top, that of Mynydd Craig-goch (1,996ft/608m). By the time you come down to A487 at Dolbenmaen you will have accomplished one of the most satisfying ridge walks in all Snowdonia (about 12 miles).

Reaching northwards into the heart of these western hills is Cwm Pennant whose beauty is celebrated by a famous poem in Welsh. Just

Moel Hebog from the north. On the right Moel Lefn drops steeply into Cwm Pennant. The conifers are part of the Forestry Commission's Beddgelert Forest before the motoring age the valley was a favourite outing from Cricieth and as you go up its narrow, jerking lane you can think of those who used to throng up here in their horse-drawn vehicles.

Beckoning irresistibly in the west above Beddgelert is the sharp peak of Moel Hebog (2,566ft/782m), one of the Park's best viewpoints because as well as having a marvellous prospect of Snowdon, Siabod, Nant Gwynant and Beddgelert, it also sees much of Lleyn and Cardigan Bay. Hebog is usually climbed from Beddgelert either from a path close to the Royal Goat Hotel or from the Forestry Commission camping ground a mile along A4805. Either way it is a walk of about 3 miles. Hebog can also be approached from the west up Cwm Llefrith or from the south from the slate quarries of Cwmystradllyn. From all directions it makes an exhilarating climb with a little final scrambling, just the expedition for a day when you don't feel quite up to taking on Snowdon. A less ambitious ascent but wholly delightful is that of Moel Ddu (1,811ft/552m) which is Hebog's neighbour to the south. It too is climbed from Cwmystradllyn or, a little more arduously, from A498 on a path that leaves the road just south of Pont Aberglaslyn.

Moel Siabod

Because it stands apart from its neighbours Moel Siabod (2,860/872m) is conspicuous from all sides. It is climbed by three main routes: in the north from the end of the Mymbyr lakes by Plas y Brenin; from the north-east at Pont Cyfyng, a mile down A5 from Capel Curig; or from the south-east at Dolwyddelan in the Lledr valley. None of the routes to this inviting peak is at all daunting, the one from Pont Cyfyng (2½ miles) probably being the easiest. Though Moel Siabod turns a solid enough face towards the north you will find it is quite hollow on the east with high corrie cliffs above a waste of scree and a shallow lake set amongst boulders. Here too are the copious remains of slate workings with a vertical face dropping sheer into a flooded quarry.

A high and empty plateau stretches for about six miles from Moel Siabod south-west to the lofty ridge of Cnicht. It is a moorland with rocky hummocks, endearing lakelets and slate quarries now silent and in ruins. Across it from west to east goes a path believed to be ancient. It starts from a bend in A498 half a mile up the road from Llyn Gwynant, climbs through woodland to a gap called Bwlch Ehediad (or Bwlch y Rhediad) and then goes boldly for 6 miles across the moors to A470 near Roman Bridge. It was evidently part of a long-distance route, for you can pick it up again where it marches onwards from Dolwyddelan to Penmachno, from where it doubtless once continued on across the rest of Wales to England. Like so many of these west-east tracks it once served as a drovers' road.

Cnicht and Moelwyn

Seen from north-west or south-east Cnicht (2,265ft/690m) is a long ridge standing high above the surrounding moorland. But from down at Porthmadog you see only the end of this narrow roof and from there it looks a real jaunty peak. Certainly on the south it is unmistakably a mountain where it plunges far into the depths of Cwm Croesor. People find their way up Cnicht by various routes, even straight up the ridge from Croesor village, which is punishment indeed. An easier approach is by way of Cwm Croesor to Croesor-fawr, then across the stream to a path which slants up the north side of the cwm. Or you can start from high up the Nantmor valley along a track that skirts round the north side of two rock-girt little lakes called Llagi and Adar, so bringing you to Cnicht from the north-east. But perhaps the most popular route of all is up Cwmorthin from Tanygrisiau, following the old road to the top quarries where the path forks right and heads across the hills for Cnicht, a walk of about 3½ miles.

Cwmorthin's deep glen is also the best gateway for the triple heights of Moelwyn and is within easy reach of the visitor centre at Tanygrisiau power-station. Because Cwmorthin is, in geographical terms, a hanging valley, the road to it climbs very steeply alongside a cascading stream. Then you are amongst the slate tips and these go with you up to Llyn Cwmorthin, a beautiful lake which at high summer is patched with yellow water-lilies. Past the lake and many ice-smoothed rocks you may think you are clear of the quarries but they begin again higher up and here the tips are even huger. Yet despite all these relics of industry Cwmorthin is slowly returning to the wildness it had in the eighteenth century when pioneer tourists wrote of its remoteness and beauty.

At the highest quarries the slopes of Moelwyn Mawr (2,527ft/770m) are clear before you, steep and toilsome but entirely rewarding, especially on some rare day of crystal clarity. For, like Hebog, this is one of the finest of all viewpoints because it enjoys fine views of Tremadog Bay as well as far inland. Facing you on the south are the broken crags of Moelwyn Bach (2,334ft/711m) but that is a height more often reached from the Stwlan reservoir. From Moelwyn Mawr you can return to Tanygrisiau by taking in the third of this group of rugged summits, Moel-yr-hydd (2,124ft/647m).

Rhinog

The spacious block of uplands that stretch south from the Vale of Ffestiniog to the Mawddach estuary make the very distinctive skyline of peaks and plunging hollows that you see from A470 near Trawsfynydd or from the coast between Barmouth and Harlech. The central and most prominent summit (though not quite the highest) is Rhinog Fawr (2,362ft/720m) and from this the whole range is usually called the Rhinogs by English visitors but is better given the Welsh form Rhinogydd. Nowhere are these wild and in places very rocky Rhinogydd crossed by motorable roads but there are several pathways all of which may date right back to antiquity; one we have already met with – the possibly Bronze Age route (10 miles) from Llanbedr to Trawsfynydd (see p 92). South of this track, and also aligned east-west, are the well-known paths from Cwm Bychan Lake up the Roman Steps and from Nantcol through the Pass of Ardudwy. Further south still a track goes from Dyffryn Ardudwy to Llyn Bodlyn which is Barmouth's water supply, and from there you can reach the southern heights of Rhinog: Diffwys (2,462ft/750m), and Y Llethr (2,475ft/754m) which is the loftiest of the whole range.

Very energetic walkers start in the north from A496 a mile or so south-west of Maentwrog and go up Ceunant Llennyrch past the long-famous Rhaeadr Ddu waterfall to the Trawsfynydd reservoir, then over one of the rockiest wildernesses in all Wales to Moel Ysgyfarnogod (2,044ft/623m) and on across the Roman Steps to Rhinog Fawr, then Rhinog Fach (2,333ft/711m) and so over the grassy domes of Y Llethr, Diffwys and Llawllech (1,930ft/588m) and down to Barmouth. A crow would say it is only fifteen miles but most people take a couple of days to do it, spending the night in or near the Artro valley. Across the south of the Rhinogydd go two roads probably built for eighteenth-century traffic. Both begin at Bont Ddu and end at Dyffryn Ardudwy, one going via Bwlch y Rhiwgyr ('drover's pass') and Pont Fadog; the other, a little to the east, passing between Llawllech and Diffwys and dropping to a charming bridge called Pont Scethin.

Ffestiniog to Arennig

The country around Manod Mawr is blessed with many pathways that once were quarry tracks or quarrymen's routes to work. And there is always Sarn Helen which will keep you good for days if you have the patience to unravel its nebulous route. Further east lies the Migneint

149

which has always been a trackless waste of bog and cotton grass and even in these drainage-mad days is still a place of lovely sog and squelch traversed mostly by naturalists while the average hill-walker skirts round it, lured onwards by the pull of Arennig Fach (2,259ft/689m) which looks across all Migneint from the east. This Arennig, its eastern cliffs dark above a corrie lake, is easily climbed from A4212 near Rhyd-y-fen (SH 826400). Or you strike due west from the northern arm of Llyn Celyn (SH 844415) which is also the starting point for a 6-mile cross-country walk northwards up and over the moors and down to Ysbyty Ifan. But this path, like those up Arennig Fach, is little used and not very easy to find.

On these hills north of Llyn Celyn we are in one of the least touristy corners of the Park where there are neither exciting peaks nor verdant vales. Instead there is a great ring of peaty moorland called Gylchedd (the name simply means 'circular') whose high point is Carnedd y Filiast which, at 2,194ft/669m), is no match for its lofty namesake on the Glyder range. Still, it has the distinction of being the most easterly outlier of Snowdonia's igneous rocks. It can be climbed by a track that winds for 3 miles north from A4212 near the car park by the reservoir dam. But you will find your route in several places is decidedly experimental.

South-west of Llyn Celyn, Arennig Fawr (2,800ft/854m) is steep, wild and rocky to the summit but is craggiest on the north and east. It is climbed from all points of the compass but perhaps most often from the west, from a ruined farmhouse called Annodd-wen which is reached along a path from the north at Rhyd-y-fen (SH 824398), close to the main road. Another, more severe ascent is from the east by way of a beautiful corrie lake, then straight up with the stream to Bwlch Blaen-y-nant. Since World War II the summit has been a place of sad memory: a memorial names the American airmen whose Flying Fortress crashed here in 1943 killing all on board. (Another war-time American plane crash is commemorated by a stone in a lay-by wall near Ynys Ettws half-way down Llanberis Pass.)

The Arennig mountains are often described as twin peaks because that is how they look from many angles. In fact there is a third, Moel Llyfnant (2,461ft/750m), close to Arennig Fawr on the south-west. An easy path up this scree-scarred dome goes north from Blaen-lliw (SH 805335) which is midway along the gated road up the Lliw valley between Llanuwchllyn and Trawsfynydd. Like all isolated uplands these summits look across vast landscapes: you see most of the mountains of north and central Wales and glimpse the sea shining off Colwyn Bay in the north and Harlech in the west.

South-west of Moel Llyfnant a 4 mile path goes up from Blaen-lliw over the forest-covered moorland and down to the Mawddach valley at Pont Aber-geirw. From there you can walk the lanes either to Trawsfynydd or Dolgellau, or find your way through the conifers of Coed y Brenin to Ganllwyd. If you want another hill climb you can carry on south to the commanding, stony heights of Rhobell Fawr (2,408ft/734m). From there you come down to Llanfachreth, one of the most charmingly sited villages in the Park. Rhobell's neighbour to the east is Dduallt (2,155ft/657m) under whose cliffs both Dee and Mawddach have their springs. Dduallt is usually climbed from Llan-uwchllyn up a track that comes up the valley south of Castell Carndochan and then skirts north of a bog called Y Fign. Dduallt sees far all round but its finest views are of the Berwyn moors, the Wnion valley and especially of Cader Idris.

The Moelwyn range from near Ffestiniog. The high-perched dam is that of Llyn Stwlan, the upper reservoir of the Tanygrisiau pumped storage power station. The highest peak is Moelwyn Mawr 2527ft (770m)

Cader Idris, Aran and Berwyn

The traditional starting point for Cader Idris (2,927ft/892m) is Dolgellau which is in the Wnion valley nearly at sea level. But to brace yourself for this rather stiff climb there are plenty of local walks to practise on. You might start with the Glen of Aran on the south of the town, or the Torrent Walk to the east. Then there is the Old Precipice Walk from Nannau (SH 7320) which circles a heathery hill and has far views down the Mawddach estuary. The New Precipice Walk which goes from Cwm yr Wnin, Llanelltyd, 2 miles west to the Mynach valley, looks straight across at Cader's great escarpment. Also from Llanelltyd you can walk all the way up Cwm yr Wnin to a Rhinog outlier called Y Garn (2,063ft/629m).

Cader Idris, with precipices, corries and lakes on both sides of its narrow ridge, has been a favourite among hill walkers every bit as long as Snowdon and, as on Snowdon, there was a time when few people dared to climb it without having the services of a guide. Today the tracks are unmistakable, the most popular being the one that starts from the car park half a mile south-west of the Gwernan Lake Hotel and zigzags you up to the summit ridge in about 1½ miles. There you turn left and walk more gently for just over a mile to the peak. Other routes come up from the south-west by way of Llanfihangel-y-pennant or, much more steeply, from Talyllyn Pass in the east. And, ever more popular in recent years, there is the Minffordd track up from the south which circles to the west high above Llyn Cau.

From Cader Idris a wilderness of mountains and moorlands stretches north-east for over thirty miles until, far beyond the limits of the Park, it drops to the deep valley of the Dee near Llangollen. Its highest point is Aran Fawddwy (2,970ft/905m), a rocky peak whose east-facing cliffs and corrie lake are the birth-place of the Dyfi. To Aran Fawddwy and its close neighbour Aran Benllyn (2,901ft/884m) there are three routes: from north, west and south. The northern one sets off from Llanuwchllyn village at SH 880297 and climbs up the end of the ridge in a series of great steps each of which deceives you into thinking that the top is in sight. The first summit, reached after 3 miles, is Aran Benllyn which is that handsome mountain you see down the length of the lake from Bala. A dip and a rise along the top of the crags and in a mile you reach Aran Fawddwy. The western route comes up through the conifers from Rhydymain and then turns left along the ridge to the peak. The path from the south is by way of Cwm Cywarch, leaving the valley road at SH 853187 for the brackeny slopes of Hengwm. It climbs to the grassy top of Dyrysgol and turns west through the pass called Drws Bach before going north to the summit. These heights of the south-east stand remote from most of the Park but they have their devotees. Aran Fawddwy is, after all, the highest mountain in Wales outside the Snowdon–Glyder–Carneddau massif.

An upland of much charm but of less renown than the Aran country lies between Cader Idris and Dinas Mawddwy. On the east side of Talyllyn Pass the broken, heathery cliffs of Craig y Llam hang with menace over A487. (There was a great rock fall on to the road here in July, 1926.) The crags along this major fault line are the shattered edge of a plateau of swelling hills which rise above the south side of A470 from Cross Foxes eastwards. For long centuries this was a land of grass and sheep but is now much beset by conifers. The north faces of several of the hills have crumbled to form cliffs or corries; and one of the summits, Mynydd Ceiswyn (SH 772139), features prominently in local geology as a widespread rock-type called the Ceiswyn Mudstones which, though thousands of feet thick, are woefully short of fossils.

A path climbs steeply eastwards from Talyllyn Pass at SH 756139 then turns south-east behind the ridge of Craig y Llam which looks north to Trawsfynydd Lake and the mountains beyond. The path was a medieval pony route from Dolgellau to Aberllefenni and, without any real evidence, has been suggested as part of the Roman road going south to Pennal. This same track from Talyllyn Pass has a branch which goes over Mynydd y Waun then drops down through the conifers into the Ratgoed valley. Cwm Ratgoed, once loud with slate quarries but now overwhelmed by forestry, is a gateway to the rest of these uplands of which Waun Oer (2,197ft/670m) is the highest. From there you can keep to the tops above the bold cirques of Craig Portas and Craig Maesglasau and come down to A470 near Dinas Mawddwy. An alternative approach to these hills goes up from the car park on A470 at the top of Bwlch Oerddrws (SH 804169).

From Dinas Mawddwy it is only 4 miles east across the hills to the boundary of the Park along the upper glen of the Dugoed stream. From the south on A458 you have a choice between two valleys, Cwm Cewydd and Cwm Clywedog. Up the Cewydd you can follow a tarmac lane for 1½ miles until it ends at the highest farm; then you turn east along a trail that with a zig and a zag gets you across the cwm, giving you views down the valley and across to the cliffs of Cwm Cywarch. As you get higher you raise the craggy summit of Aran Fawddwy and have an unequalled vista of the upper Dyfi valley. The track is now a delicious green road high above the Dyfi and so it goes on until you see another alluring green road coming up the east bank of the Clywedog. Before you is a world of grassy uplands reaching to the horizon with never a bare rock in sight: but it is being sadly invaded by conifers. From here you can go north along a track that slips between a low hill called Ffridd Ddu and a bolder one called Y Foel, and you are soon down to the Dyfi. Alternatively, you can go south down the Clywedog and back to A458 near Llidiart y Barwn (Baron's Gate), a spot still remembered for the murder in 1555 of a local potentate, Baron Lewis Owen, by the Gwylliaid Cochion Mawddwy ('the red-headed bandits of Mawddwy').

This south-eastern corner of the Park can also be reached by foot-paths from Dinas Mawddwy and Aber-cywarch. But the Park's border-land a few miles north is best approached from the pass of Bwlch-y-groes. Up there we are at the western end of the far-reaching Berwyn moorlands whose major summits are outside the Park to the east. Within the Park one of the highest is Foel y Geifr (2,054ft/626m) which can be climbed from three directions: along the Park boundary from Bwlch-y-groes (3½ miles); up the Rhyd-wen valley from Llangywair (also 3½ miles); or from the top of Cwm Hirnant, 2 miles north-west of the tip of Lake Vyrnwy. East from Hirnant the watershed, and with it the Park boundary, go on at a high level as far as the Bala-Welshpool road at the strangely named Milltir Gerrig ('stony mile'). The valleys below, centred on Rhos-y-gwaliau, are largely given over to the conifers of the Penllyn (Aberhirnant) plantations and there are miles of forest walks.

South of Cader Idris

The coastal region from the Mawddach to the Dysynni has long been crossed by footpaths. In Chapter 5 we traced a possible Bronze Age route north-east from Aberdysynni to link with Ffordd Ddu, the ancient road which, perhaps after serving a term as a Roman road, eventually became a coaching road from Dolgellau to Tywyn. From maps you will easily pick out other trails. A favourite one goes steeply up from Friog past a charming woodland waterfall and over to the Cregennen lakes. Just before the fall you can turn right and climb past deserted slate workings to look down at the remarkable Blue Lake, a deeply flooded quarry whose water looks like a strong solution of copper sulphate. From there you can also get to the Cregennen lakes or find your way back down to the coast. All the broad slopes above Llwyngwril are even and grassy because they are deep in glacial drift which has buried the surface rocks and hidden any irregularities that may have

154

ruffled the original surface. This smoothness makes for excellent walking country and the many trails across it have wide views over the sea to Lleyn and Bardsey Island.

Ever-spreading conifer plantations impinge hugely on the scene in the most southerly section of the Park which lies between the Dysynni and Dyfi valleys. But the highest ridges such as Tarren-y-gesail (2,186ft/666m) and Tarren Hendre (2,076ft/633m) still stand clear of the forests; and we must hope that all the old trackways will not be obliterated by the spruces, especially the one which goes for 6 miles up from Abergynolwyn and over Pont Llaeron to Machynlleth or alternatively to Pennal. Tarren-y-gesail can be climbed from Abergynolwyn, Pennal, Machynlleth, Pantperthog or Corris Uchaf (Upper Corris). To Tarren Hendre the most direct approach is from the north at Dolgoch Falls. The lower hills further west can be reached by many delightful paths from Aberdyfi, Tywyn or Cwm Maethlon.

GAZETTEER

Aberdyfi (SN 6195)   At the southern tip of the Park this popular yachting and holiday resort (a busy little port in pre-railway days) looks south across the Dyfi estuary to the woods and gentle hills of Ceredigion. The view to the west is over a golf course and dunes to Cardigan Bay. Along the estuary road is the Outward Bound Sea School where young people are taught the art of self-reliance on various adventure courses. On the waterfront is the Outward Bound sailing museum and a National Park information centre. There are walks with far views on the hills above the village or over to Cwm Maethlon (Happy Valley) and Llyn Barfog (Bearded Lake).

Aberglaslyn Pass (SH 5946)   Aberglaslyn has been a Mecca ever since tourism began, the favourite view of the precipitous gorge being upstream from the single-arched stone bridge over the Glaslyn. A popular walk is from Nantmor up to Beddgelert (1½ miles) along the old narrow-gauge track which includes an exciting ¼ mile tunnel. The tides used to come up to Aberglaslyn before the building of Porthmadog embankment.

Abergwyngregyn (SH 6572)   Often simply called Aber, this small village is close to but hidden from the main road between Bangor and Llanfairfechan. It early became a centre for tourists wishing to see the waterfall that comes roaring over a cliff 2 miles up the valley to the south. Until the Menai was bridged in 1826 the traffic from England to Ireland took a direct route from here across the Lavan Sands at low water to get the ferry to Beaumaris, a hair-raising venture if a spring tide came in with a gale behind it. For travellers coming from Beaumaris a great bell was tolled at Aber church to guide them across the sands on foggy days.

Aber also has links with a remoter past. A thirteenth-century castle mound (Pen y Mwd) is traditionally linked with the princes of Gwynedd. Across the valley went a Roman road from Segontium (Caernarfon) to Canovium (Caerhun). Further up is Maes y Gaer, an Iron Age hill fort, and higher still are other prehistoric settlements. Aber is a starting point for the long climb to Foel Fras, most northerly of Snowdonia's 3,000-footers. The route takes you up past the well-watered woodlands of a national nature reserve.

Abergynolwyn (SH 6706) A former slate-quarry village in the Dysynni valley 6 miles upstream from Tywyn and near the terminus of the Talyllyn Railway. Within easy reach are Bird Rock, Castell y Bere, Llanfihangel-y-pennant, Talyllyn Lake and the Bryneglwys quarries (abandoned 1947). A museum in the village tells the story of slate.

Aberhirnant (SH 9533) Also called Penllyn, this is a large and increasing Forestry Commission conifer forest south-east of Bala. A motor road goes right through it from Rhos-y-gwaliau up Cwm Hirnant and down to Lake Vyrnwy. A picnic site and forest trails are available.

Aran range (SH 8622) Aran Fawddwy and Aran Benllyn, 9 miles east-north-east of Dolgellau, are the twin tops of this commanding ridge which links the Berwyn range with Cader Idris to form one of the great upland barriers across Wales. Aran Fawddwy looks east down steep cliffs to Craiglyn, the source lake of the Dyfi. There are paths up from Llanuwchllyn in the north, Cwm Cywarch in the south and Rhydymain in the west.

Arennig range (SH 8237) Six miles west of Bala the twin Arennig peaks show up boldly from all round. They are wild with rocks and heather and both have a corrie lake shadowed under east-facing crags. Intermediate in height between the two is their close neighbour, Moel Llyfnant.

Arthog (SH 6414) A village strung out along A493 south of the Mawddach estuary between Penmaenpool and Fairbourne, Arthog is a starting point for Cader Idris. The lane begins up a wooded, waterfall-loud glen and climbs to the twin Cregennen lakes (National Trust) with their lovely mountain views. (This lane is narrow, winding and gated, and motorists should approach the lakes from Dolgellau not Arthog.) Between Arthog and the estuary is a wild, boggy tract (crossed by footpaths) of interest to naturalists for its wildflowers and insects. There is also walking and pony-trekking along the old railway track between Penmaenpool and Morfa Mawddach station.

Bala (SH 9236) Bala dates from the Middle Ages and its wide, straight main street suggests Norman town planning. The castle mound, Tomen y Bala, survives almost in the town centre. Otherwise medieval Bala has vanished, the houses being mostly Victorian or modern with a few Georgian. The eastern gateway to the Park, Bala is one of the most Welsh-speaking towns. Drop in on market day (Thursday) and listen to the farming folk. This very rural little town stands at the head of a magnificent lake with wild uplands all round – Arennig, Aran and Berwyn. In the north the Celyn reservoir and the Tryweryn river with its white-water canoeing are within easy reach; so is Lake Vyrnwy in the south. An eighteenth-century tourist, Lord Lyttleton, commented: 'What Bala is most famous for is the beauty of its women; I saw there some of the prettiest girls I ever beheld.'

Bala Lake (Llyn Tegid) (SH 9033) 4 miles long, this is the largest natural lake in Wales and is owned by the Park Authority. It is rich in fish and is much used for angling and sailing (but no power-boats). A narrow-gauge railway runs for 4½ miles along the south bank. A village along the railway is Llangywair (Llangower) which has a picnic place and car park close to the water's edge. There is an attractive old church with a rare survival, a horse-bier, inside. Nearby Glyn Gywair is a route up to the Berwyn moors. North of the lake is the village of Y Parc, a good stepping-off place for Arennig Fawr.

Bangor (SH 5871) Three miles outside the Park, Bangor is a mainly Victorian and modern city at the north-east end of the Menai Strait and has long been known to travellers between London and Holyhead. The higher parts of the town have views to Anglesey in the north-west and of a spectacular line of mountains in the south. Bangor is a university town (since 1883) and also a holiday, yachting, sea-angling and shopping centre. The High Street is pedestrianised and there is a Friday open-air market. There is an attractive pier and a harbour near to which was Port Penrhyn, terminus of the former narrow-gauge railway which brought the slate down from Bethesda.

In the centre the site of the cathedral may date back to the fifth-century St Deiniol; and the name Bangor (originally Bangor Deiniol) also goes back that far. It means a wattle fence such as presumably enclosed Deiniol's original monastery or seminary. The cathedral (nineteenth century with fragments back to the fourteenth century) contains many interesting features and memorials, and there is a Biblical Garden on the north side. Across the road a museum and art gallery exhibits many centuries of Welsh history. The town hall was a Tudor Bishop's Palace, now very much altered. Theatre Gwynedd is a first-class small, modern theatre with a restaurant. Bangor is a good centre for visiting Penrhyn Castle, Aber Falls, Nant Ffrancon, Cwm Idwal and the Glyder and Carneddau uplands.

Barmouth (SH 6115) In Welsh, Y Bermo. Formerly a small port and ship-building centre, Barmouth became popular when eighteenth-century invalids flocked here because doctors proclaimed the health-giving effects of sea-bathing. The patients were also fed on scurvy-grass (full of vitamin C) from the Mawddach estuary. It was not until the coming of the railway that the town became a playground for the general public (chiefly Midlanders) attracted by the miles of sands and the splendid scenery.

Modern Barmouth, with its many Victorian and more recent guest-houses and hotels, is squeezed tightly between a mountainside and the sea and many of its buildings are staged high above the main street. The famous railway viaduct can be well seen from the quayside. Here a few buildings survive from former days including a circular lock-up for drunken sailors. There is also a Maritime Museum (RNLI). Among popular outings are the Panorama Walk which looks up the estuary to Cader Idris; the path along the railway bridge to Arthog; and the ferry over the rivermouth to Fairbourne.

158

Penrhyn Castle near Bangor. Now in the care of the National Trust and open to the public, this pseudo-medieval castle, on an ancient site, was built in the early nineteenth century out of the huge profits of the Penrhyn slate quarries at Bethesda

Beddgelert (SH 5948)   Twelve-miles south-east of Caernarfon, Beddgelert is a village among the mountains. It has long been a tourist centre not only for climbing Snowdon or Moel Hebog but also for anglers and people who come to see Aberglaslyn Pass, the track of the former Welsh Highland Railway, the old copper mines, the ancient fort of Dinas Emrys and the beauties of Nant Gwynant and the Nantmor valley. In its plantations on Hebog's slopes the Forestry Commission has a large and well-appointed camping and caravan site (SH 578491) and a car park and picnic site with trails (SH 573508). Both are along A4085, the road to Caernarfon. The parish church is on the site of a long-vanished Augustinian priory. It is nineteenth century with thirteenth-century fragments such as the east window and the arcade in the north transept.

The name Beddgelert ('grave of Gelert') probably refers to some holy man of the Dark Ages. Certainly the alleged grave of the faithful hound, Gelert, on the south side of the village, is totally spurious. All the same it has successfully taken in the tourists of two hundred years.

Bethesda (SH 6266)   A town 4 miles south-east of Bangor along A5. The biblical name, dating from 1840, is that of a Nonconformist chapel which was the centre

159

of Bethesda's then newly-formed community. The religious revival inspired many similar place-names: Ebenezer, Bethania, Carmel, Caesarea, Nebo, Siloam and so on. Bethesda is a quarrying town of little charm but there is plenty of drama in its setting. Adjacent are the immense workings where slate is still being won and further back is a heart-stirring prospect of the Carneddau and Glyder ranges separated by the deep trench of Nant Ffrancon. On foot from Bethesda you can be on the top of Carnedd Dafydd in about three hours and then go along the cliff-tops of Ysgolion Duon (the Black Ladders) to Carnedd Llywelyn. From Bethesda by car it is only a few minutes to Ogwen, setting-off place for Cwm Idwal, Tryfan and all the Glyder summits. Along a lane half-way between Bethesda and Bangor is Cochwillan (SH 606694), a well-preserved fifteenth-century hall that is viewable by appointment.

Betws-y-coed (SH 7856)   Long dedicated to tourism, this is a large village with many hotels, guest houses and shops; and being on A5 its traffic is very heavy. It is beautifully placed where woods and streams unite in a world of cool, green glens that are loud with cataracts and waterfalls, notably the Swallow Falls 2 miles up the Llugwy. Old stone bridges stride the Llugwy, Conwy and Lledr rivers, and there is also the famous iron Waterloo Bridge which Telford built across the Conwy in 1815. Spanning the Llugwy is the Miners' Bridge, a curiously sloping, wooden structure which used to link the village with now defunct lead mines. Public footpaths radiate in all directions to wooded glens and streamsides and there are also walks and nature trails in the Forestry Commission's Gwydyr Forest which covers many of the nearby slopes and moors. For details of them all consult the information and interpretative centre in the heart of the village at Y Stablau, where there is an audio-visual theatre, a craft display and an aquarium.

Betws-y-coed is old. The name, meaning 'the oratory in the forest', is medieval and so in part is the parish church with its fine fourteenth-century stone effigy of Gruffydd ap Dafydd Goch in studded armour. The railway which rather unexpectedly survives up to Blaenau Ffestiniog has a station at Betws-y-coed and near the station is the Conwy Valley railway museum.

Blaenau Ffestiniog (SH 7045)   This is a mainly nineteenth-century slate quarrying town at the head of the Vale of Ffestiniog. These days the old industry has largely died away and the vast quarries have turned into tourist attractions: the Llechwedd Slate Caverns and the Gloddfa Ganol mountain centre. At both you can explore the mines and quarries and learn all about their history and technology. You can go by bus to see the Tanygrisiau pumped storage power-station, including its higher reservoir, Llyn Stwlan, which is far up the slopes of Moelwyn Mawr; or by the narrow gauge railway to Porthmadog; or by main-line train to Betws-y-coed or Llandudno. A restored eighteenth-century fulling mill at Tanygrisiau is a reminder of the rural past. Walkers will find many paths to the local woods, rivers and waterfalls and the heights of Moelwyn and Manod. There is also a very interesting town trail and a Park information centre.

Bodnant Garden (SH 801723)   Near A470, 6 miles south of Llandudno, the garden is one of the National Trust's finest properties and is famous for its lovely rhododendrons, camellias, magnolias and many other shrubs and trees. There are beautiful views across the Conwy valley to the Carneddau uplands.

Bont Ddu (SH 6718) This is a beautifully-placed village above the Mawddach estuary between Dolgellau and Barmouth. At Pont Hirgwm 1 mile up the lane north-west, a Park notice board tells the story of the local gold mines. In another mile the lane divides into two alluring trackways which go away over the hills and down to Dyffryn Ardudwy, one via Pont Fadog, the other over Pont Scethin. Close to Bont Ddu in the west are the estuaryside woods of Farch Ynys with picnic site and walks.

Bwlch Drws Ardudwy (SH 6628) This is a pass between Rhinog Fawr and Rhinog Fach connecting the Trawsfynydd district with Ardudwy in the west, and no doubt it was often guarded and fortified in troublesome times. Like Bwlch Tyddiad a mile north, it is a rough and rocky way and there are a few ancient paving slabs on the west side that are reminiscent of the Roman Steps. Thomas Pennant noted these slabs when he was here in 1773. His Romantic soul was clearly much impressed: 'I was tempted to visit this noted pass and found the horror of it far exceeding the most gloomy idea that could be conceived of it. The sides seem to have been rent by some mighty convulsion into a thousand pre-cipices . . .'

Cader Idris (SH 7013) Though there are many higher summits in the Park, Cader (or Cadair) Idris has always been a favourite because of its great cliffs on either side of a narrow ridge that looks down upon corrie lakes set in a wild scene of rocks and screes. Cader stands up in magnificent isolation because deep valleys have developed along strong fault-lines north and south (the Mawddach and Talyllyn troughs). You can climb it from the four points of the compass but most people go up from the north from the car park a mile south-west of Llyn Gwernan, following the old pony track that went over to Llanfihangel-y-pennant. Others go up from the south from Minffordd by way of Llyn Cau. Masochists go up Foxes Path from Llyn Gwernan, struggling up loose scree much of the way. The name of this much-cherished mountain means the fortress (or seat) of Idris, a hero or giant of legend. Cader is celebrated amongst geologists, geographers and botanists and is a national nature reserve much visited by students.

Caerhun (SH 7770) Five miles south of Conwy, this was the site of the Roman fort of Canovium, comfortably placed on the Conwy estuary. The fort has long ago disappeared but its rectangle of banks is still clear to see and Roman roads are partly traceable east, west and south. A medieval church occupies a corner of the Roman site. Note the eighteenth-century lychgate with mounting block and tethering ring.

Caernarfon (SH 4762) A very historic town, formerly a port, now a yachting and tourist centre on the Menai Strait, 5 miles north-west of the Park. Its major attraction is the castle (built 1285–1322) which is notable for its many towers and immense walls. In 1660 Charles II signed an order for its demolition but for some unknown reason this was ignored. All the same the castle is but an empty shell, its interior being mostly lawns, but it serves well for royal occasions.

Caernarfon is the most magnificent of all Edward I's castles but most of the interior buildings have disappeared. The King's Gate and the Eagle Tower are among the chief features of this thirteenth century castle

---

Among Caernarfon's other attractions are the town walls, built at the same time as the castle, and the street pattern surviving within them; the museum of the Royal Welch Fusiliers (at the castle); the Georgian buildings in the town centre; the yacht-filled harbour; and the site of Roman Segontium and its very good museum. Close to the Roman fort is the partly thirteenth-century church of Llanbeblig which stands where the Romans had their pre-Christian church, a temple dedicated to Mithras, the special god of Roman soldiers. The present-day cemetery is on the site of the Roman burial ground. Llanbeblig church has magnificent roof timbers, medieval cross slabs and an elaborate sixteenth-century alabaster altar tomb. Two miles south-west of Caernarfon at Llanfaglan another church has survived from the Middle Ages. It is unrestored and retains its eighteenth-century seating and lychgate as well as a Dark Ages inscribed stone.

Capel Curig (SH 7158) A far-flung village on A5, 5 miles west of Betws-y-coed. It was put on the tourist map by Lord Penrhyn when he made a road through Nant Ffrancon to get the slates from his Bethesda quarry to the English Midlands (c 1790). At Capel Curig he built 'a spacious hotel' (the Royal) which is now Plas y Brenin, the National Mountaineering Centre where you can learn all about climbing, skiing, canoeing and other upland skills. Just west along A4806 are the twin Mymbyr lakes, foreground of a classic view of Snowdon.

Mercifully, though long a popular starting point for the Glyder and Carneddau ranges and for Moel Siabod, Capel Curig has never grown into a brash tourist centre. There are hotels, guest houses and a few sports, craft and other shops. But the feeling is always of being very close to the open moors with greater heights not far away.

Capel Garmon (SH 8155)   Winding lanes lead up to this village 2 miles east-south-east of Betws-y-coed and known for its well-preserved Neolithic chambered tomb ½ mile south. Originally it was a long barrow complete with entrance passage, false door and three burial chambers but only one of these has kept its massive capstone.

Carneddau Hengwm (SH 613205)   Most of the prehistoric cairns on the Welsh uplands are circular and marked Bronze Age burials; but a few cairns have survived from an earlier time, the Neolithic or New Stone Age, and may be recognised by their elongated shape. Among them are the twin Carneddau Hengwm long cairns on a shelf of the hills 3 miles north of Barmouth. Though much despoiled for wall building they are still well worth visiting. Probably both these cairns contained several burial chambers. Not far away are relics of the Bronze and Iron Ages, making this a very rewarding area for archaeologists.

Carneddau range   This is the spacious high moorland stretching north-east from Nant Ffrancon to the lower Conwy. It is a grassy and in places stony plateau that

---

The art of canoeing is one of the skills taught at Plas y Brenin, Capel Curig, the National Centre for Mountain Activities where many other outdoor pursuits are also catered for

dips and rises from summit to summit and includes Carnedd Llywelyn and Carnedd Dafydd which, after Snowdon and Crib y Ddysgl, are the highest British
mountains south of the Grampians. The names Llywelyn and Dafydd no doubt
commemorate heroes of long ago. The other Carneddau 3,000-footers are Pen-yr-
ole-wen, Foel Grach, Yr Elen and Foel Fras.

On several sides the Carneddau break off into great cliffs or vertiginous screes,
notably Craig Braich Tu Du above Nant Ffrancon; Ysgolion Duon at the head of
Cwm Llafar; Craig y Dulyn and Craig-fawr on the east side of Foel Grach; Craig
yr Ysfa which looks down Cwm Eigiau; and the crags around Cwm Lloer. The Carneddau are blessed with fine lakes, all in wild mountainy settings. Most of these
uplands are well above the tree zone and so have escaped being smothered by
conifers except on the lower slopes towards Betws-y-coed.

Castell Prysor (SH 758369) The Park is scattered with medieval castle
mounds of little history, many of them once crowned by wooden towers within
palisades. Prysor Castle, prominent on a rock above the Prysor stream 3 miles east
of Trawsfynydd, was a stone tower but hardly anything remains of it. No doubt it
was intended to command this vital east-west pass in early Norman times. Near
it runs the abandoned Bala-Ffestiniog railway.

Castell y Bere (SH 6608) The remains of this hill-top castle are in the Dysynni
valley 6 miles north-east of Tywyn. Originally Welsh, it was taken by Edward I
who rebuilt it and hoped to create a borough there in 1285. But ten years later the
Welsh rose in rebellion, the castle was destroyed and the borough never
developed.

Coed y Brenin Begun in 1922 this large Forestry Commission plantation in the
Dolgellau area occupies much of the Mawddach and Wnion valleys. Besides
various trails and picnicking places a special feature is the excellent visitor centre
at Maesgwm, 5 miles north of Dolgellau. From the earliest days of tourism this
region was popular not only for the attractions of Cader Idris and the Mawddach
estuary but also for three famous waterfalls. One is Rhaeadr Ddu on the National
Trust property at Ganllwyd. The other two are Rhaeadr Mawddach and Pistyll
Cain which are close together where two rivers meet near Gwynfynydd gold mine
in the heart of the forest (SH 7327). The name Coed y Brenin means 'The King's
Wood' and commemorates the Silver Jubilee of King George V in 1935.

Conwy (SH 7777) A small estuaryside town famous for its castle and marvell-
ously complete medieval town walls, Conwy is the best surviving example of a
fortified town in Britain. At the north apex of the Park and served by A55 and the
London–Holyhead railway, it is a perfect base for visits to north Snowdonia. Its
strategic position has been appreciated ever since the Iron Age, when the top of
Conwy Mountain was chosen as the site of a fort that is noteworthy for its many
hut circles and for its wide views all round. In the thirteenth-century along came
Edward I with his plans of conquest and he chose to build one of his great castles
at Conwy.

Among other notable buildings are St Mary's church, a product of various
centuries, the fourteenth-century south transept being especially fine. There is

a restored sixteenth-century wooden rood screen beautifully decorated with
fauna and flora. The fifteenth-century stall ends are likewise well carved and there
are interesting memorials, old and modern. Plas Mawr is an elegantly decorated
Elizabethan house open to the public and is now an art gallery. Climb its stairs for
a roof-top view of the town. Another well-preserved house, Aberconwy (sixteenth century), is owned by the National Trust. At Gyffyn, half a mile south-
west of the castle, the little church has a fifteenth-century ceiling painted with
saintly portraits and there are quaint medieval carvings in the porch.

Corris (SH 7507)   As you go north from Machynlleth along the winding A487
you follow the course of the former narrow-gauge railway built to bring slate from
the mines and quarries of Corris and Aberllefenni (SH 7709) to what was then
the little Dyfi port of Derwenlas. Though slate-working has ceased at Corris it
continues at Aberllefenni. On the main road between Corris Uchaf and Corris
Isaf (Upper and Lower Corris) are craft shops selling a wide range of local work
including many things made from slate. Corris is a good base for climbing Tarren
y Gesail and Cader Idris. From Aberllefenni an ancient path goes north-west over
the hills and down to Dolgellau. Up Cwm Ratgoed you can reach the hills west of
Dinas Mawddwy. A forest road goes east through the plantations of the Dyfi Forest
6 miles to Aberangell. Close to Aberllefenni there is a Forestry Commission
picnic area and a trail.

Craig yr Aderyn (Bird Rock), site of a unique colony of cormorants whose nests
are in the cliffs (partly in shadow) towards the left of the picture

Craig yr Aderyn (SH 6406)   Known in English as Bird Rock, this high, north-facing crag has been known for at least three centuries for its unique colony of inland-nesting cormorants, about forty pairs of which breed here 4 miles from the sea and are quite a spectacle as they come in far overhead, gliding down to the cliff ledges. Possibly they have bred here since the days of prehistory when the daily tides used to wash the foot of Craig yr Aderyn. A footpath to the summit leads you through the ruined walls of an Iron Age fort to a panorama of the Dysynni valley from the sea to Cader Idris with the fields below spread out as in an aerial photograph.

Crib Goch (SH 6255)   You set out along the Pig Track from Pen-y-pass, go round the foot of the first rocky buttress and there before you is this tall, sharp peak. Perhaps nowhere, except on Tryfan, is the walker so closely involved with bare rock as here on Crib Goch. From its sharp ridge you scramble down to the col called Bwlch Coch whence you can either carry on up to Crib y Ddysgl, turn right down into Cwm Glas-mawr or left down a cruel scree to rejoin the Pig Track.

Croesor (SH 6244)   This is a very small, former slate-quarrying village tucked away in a deep valley under the screes of Cnicht. There is a car park nearby from which walks go up Cnicht or to the Moelwyn summits. The quarry (or rather mine) was at the head of the cwm down which a nineteenth-century tramway took the slates to Porthmadog.

Cwm Bychan, Llanbedr (SH 6431)   Five miles up the beautifully wooded Artro valley is a fine mountain hollow with a deep-looking lake shadowed by echoing cliffs. From here you look intimately up to the great stony terraces of the north end of Rhinog which you can easily climb by way of the Roman Steps. But the narrow lane that wriggles its way up the Artro from Llanbedr can be a motorists' nightmare at high summer.

Cwm Bychan, Nantmor (SH 6046)   From the car park near Aberglaslyn Bridge a popular footpath takes you up this narrow valley (National Trust) past copper mine relics to a fine viewpoint called Moel y Dyniewyd and down to Llyn Dinas in Nant Gwynant.

Cwm Dyli (SH 6354)   Erosion has attacked Snowdon on a grand scale, hollowing its flanks into spectacular corries like Cwm Dyli which lies deep between the outstretched arms of the Snowdon Horseshoe. The Park's highest and rockiest ridges form the skyline at the head of this great cwm; and the corrie lakes, Glaslyn and Llyn Llydaw, are overhung by the precipices of Lliwedd, Clogwyn y Garnedd and Crib Goch. Cwm Dyli has not always been the uninhabited place it is today: you can still see the ruins of barracks and other buildings dating back to the copper mining days of the eighteenth and nineteenth centuries.

Cwm Idwal (SH 6459)   This fine corrie, hollowed out of the east flank of the Glyder range, is reached after about twenty minutes easy walking from Ogwen Cottage. You go over a low ridge and there before you is one of the classic mountain-scapes of Snowdonia – the shapely tarn, Llyn Idwal, below its great cliffs whose rock beds exhibit a beautifully symmetrical downward arch (syncline) in the strata. This arch is split by Twll Du ('black chasm'), long called the Devil's Kitchen by English tourists. From a lake above (Llyn y Cwn) a stream tumbles spectacularly through the Kitchen and down to Llyn Idwal. It is up this chasm that you have to scramble to reach the moorland above. Once there you can turn left for Glyder Fawr or right for Y Garn.

Cwm Pennant (SH 5347) This is the celebrated valley of the Dwyfor which flows to the sea 1 mile west of Cricieth Castle. Near its banks as you go upstream are Lloyd George's grave at Llanystumdwy and a Neolithic burial chamber at Rhoslan (SH 483409). All round the upper Pennant valley the hill shapes are inviting and there are fine ridge walks. Traces of Iron Age settlements are frequent on these uplands; so are relics of modern quarries and mines. Surviving improbably is a great water-wheel brought from Cornwall to work the copper mine in Cwm Ciprwth (SH 526478).

Cwmystradllyn (SH 5644) This is a happy hunting ground for industrial history enthusiasts. Here nineteenth-century quarrying has bequeathed a big, imposing ruin that looks down the bare moorland valley like some monument of ancient Rome. In it was dressed the slate brought down from the hills, the machinery powered by water from the nearby lake. Up past the lake you can find your way to two noble heights, Moel Ddu and Moel Hebog.

Deganwy (SH 7779) Just south of Llandudno, this yachting and holiday centre shelters from the east winds at the mouth of the estuary opposite Conwy. On the hill above are the scanty ruins of a castle which saw much of the bloody side of life when the Anglo-Normans invaded Wales. Built by the English in 1211 it was eventually destroyed by Llywelyn the Last in 1263. Twenty years later Edward I began his castle at Conwy and a new stage of conquest had started.

Dinas Emrys (SH 606492) The fame of this ancient monument on a wooded hill overlooking Llyn Dinas 1 mile along A498 from Beddgelert rests on its links with a Welsh legend. It began as an Iron Age hill fort which continued in use through and after the Roman period. In the fifth century, according to tradition, the British leader, Vortigern, took refuge here from the invading Saxons. All that can be seen today are the castle mound and base walls of a twelfth-century keep that was evidently similar to those still standing at Dolbadarn and Dolwyddelan – built by the Welsh to defend Snowdonia from the English. The site was excavated in the 1950s.

Dinas Mawddwy (SH 8514) A centre of local power in the Middle Ages, Dinas Mawddwy, 8 miles east of Dolgellau, is a quiet village close to A470. Formerly busy with quarries and mines it is now more involved with farming and forestry. At the old railway station (there used to be a line to Machynlleth) you can see cloth being woven at Meirion Mill where there is a visitor centre, craft shop and café. Nearby is a picturesque old pack-horse bridge. Dinas Mawddwy lies deep between the hills and is a gateway both to the Mynydd Ceiswyn group of uplands and to the upper Dyfi country which climbs to the Aran range and is a land of high

The view is up the narrowing Dyfi valley from near Dinas Mawddwy to the moorlands that link the Aran and Berwyn ranges

---

rocks, rivers and waterfalls. To the north a steep, narrow but motorable road takes you up to the high pass of Bwlch-y-groes which has a grand view of Arennig. Up there you can turn right for Lake Vyrnwy or go straight on down the Twrch valley to Llanuwchllyn and Bala.

Dinorwig hydro-electric scheme (SH 5959)   This pumped storage installation near Llanberis, mainly hidden underground, utilises two lakes, the higher one being Llyn Marchlyn Mawr and the lower Llyn Peris, and their levels fluctuate accordingly.

Dolbenmaen (SH 5043)   A small village, Dolbenmaen is situated at the point where A487 crosses the Dwyfor stream 5 miles north-west of Tremadog. Across the road from the little fifteenth-century church, the medieval castle mound may have been the site of the precursor of Cricieth Castle. Up a lane 1 mile north-east is the well-known Brynkir woollen mill. The tree-surrounded stone tower on a nearby hill is a nineteenth-century folly.

Dolgellau (SH 7217)   This old stone-built town in the Wnion valley 10 miles inland from Barmouth has been a popular centre since the earliest days of tourism. Though its buildings of the Middle Ages have all gone its layout of narrow streets round a square could well be as medieval as the effigy of the knight lying in the parish church. The stone bridge over the river is seventeenth century and the nearby tannery looks as old. Dolgellau is the administrative centre and market town for a large area and is a bastion of Welsh culture with strong links with the career of Owain Glyndwr. It is the most usual starting point for Cader Idris and there are many shorter walks in the neighbourhood including Torrent Walk, Precipice Walk and the Glen of Aran. Tal-y-waen farm along the Cader Road welcomes visitors who wish to see sheep-farming in action and also has a nature trail and picnic area. There is a Park information centre in the town. Of interest to industrial archaeologists is the early eighteenth-century charcoal blast-furnace at Dolgun, 1½ miles east of Dolgellau (SH 751187). (Enquire at Fronalchen caravan park.)

Dolwyddelan (SH 7252)   This village lies in the beautiful Lledr valley half-way between Betws-y-coed and Blaenau Ffestiniog. It has two noteworthy buildings – a conspicuous thirteenth-century castle and a modest sixteenth-century church which has its original rood screen, a fine painted memorial tablet (seventeenth century) with heraldic shields, and other interesting features. Several ancient roads cross the country hereabouts: a Roman road comes up from Caerhun; a medieval (or earlier) track goes west to Nant Gwynant and east to Penmachno. Between here and Blaenau Ffestiniog is the Crimea Pass with a distant view of Snowdon on the way up.

Dyffryn Ardudwy (SH 5823)   A straggling, near-coastal built-up area 5 miles north of Barmouth on A496. A mile west is a long sandy shore and there are many caravans. The dunelands of Morfa Dyffryn are a national nature reserve. Inland rises the Rhinog range with infinite scope for hill walking. Antiquities dating right back to the Neolithic Age are frequent in the district, the nearest being two burial chambers in the village itself just behind the school at SH 588228.

Dyfi (Dovey) Forest (SH 7708)   This is the most southern of the Forestry Commission's plantations in Snowdonia and is partly within and partly outside the Park. Included in it are some of the slopes of Tarren y Gesail and neighbouring hills. Here there are fine moorland walks going over high viewpoint ridges from Machynlleth or Pennal to Abergynolwyn or Dolgoch Falls. Also within the Park are those parts of Dyfi Forest that lie between Aberllefenni and Dinas Mawddwy, a region of high, wild country well worth rambling over. There are picnic sites and forest trails at Aberllefenni (SH 769093) and near Pantperthog (SH 755054). Most of the trees are the usual conifers but there are also some fine stands of southern beech (*Nothofagus*) from South America.

Eryri   The Welsh name for Snowdonia. It is of doubtful meaning but it could be related to the Greek *oros*, a mountain; and it may be no coincidence that one of the highest settlements in Wales is a hilltop hamlet called Eryrys above Llanarmon-yn-Iâl in Clwyd.

Fairbourne (SH 6112)   A residential and holiday village on the south side of the Mawddach estuary, Fairbourne has dunes and long bathing sands. A 15-in gauge

The Vale of Ffestiniog still has many of the oakwoods for which it has long been celebrated and several are nature reserves. There are many public paths through the woods. The mountain in the background is Manod Mawr

miniature railway opened early this century to carry materials to build the village now takes passengers on its 2 miles of track that ends at the Barmouth ferry. There are walks inland up through woods to local waterfalls and old quarries, or further afield to the Cregennen lakes and Cader Idris. There is also a footpath to Barmouth along the railway viaduct. Still intact defences against Hitler's tanks suggest that Fairbourne has not yet accepted that World War II is over.

Ffestiniog, Vale of (SH 6640)   The Vale is a place of complete contrast between the workaday town of Blaenau Ffestiniog at the head and the lovely Dwyryd valley below with its woodlands and waterfalls. The biggest (almost town-sized) village is Ffestiniog whose origins long pre-date Blaenau, a town entirely of the industrial revolution. Three miles down the Vale, Maentwrog ('stone of Twrog') gets its name from a rough boulder outside the west end of the church. Though long believed to have been placed there in memory of the Dark Ages saint, Twrog, it is more likely to be a glacial deposit. The mansion on the opposite hill is Pas Tan-y-bwlch. Ancient farmhouses add to the attractions of this Vale.

Ffwrnais (Furnace) (SN 6895)   Just outside the Park on the south this village on A487, 7 miles south-west of Machynlleth, has a recently restored iron smeltery of the eighteenth century which was built on the site of a seventeenth-century silver-lead refinery. The machinery was powered by the stream that comes down the beautiful Cwm Einion (Artists' Valley). Across the road is the entrance to the RSPB's Ynys-hir reserve, and on the hill above the furnace an RSPB trail goes up to a viewpoint (with *table d'orientation*) which looks across the wide Dyfi estuary to the bold southern ramparts of Snowdonia.

Friog (SH 6112)   A hamlet on the Cardigan Bay coast road (A493), Friog is ½ mile south of Fairbourne. The Cambrian Coast Railway from here south to Llwyngwril looks rather precariously perched on its narrow shelf above the sea cliffs. Railway enthusiasts might enjoy the walk along the beach here at low tide to see the extensive walls built to shore up the crumbling cliffs.

Ganllwyd (SH 7224)   This village, well-known to anglers, is on A470 4 miles north of Dolgellau. It is now rather engulfed in the conifers of Coed y Brenin but there used to be much more broad-leaved woodland here, some of which survives on the National Trust's Dolmelynllyn estate. Here the Gamlan stream, rising high up the slopes of Y Llethr, comes in haste down through the woods and throws itself over a long-famous fall called Rhaeadr Ddu. Two other falls, Pistyll Cain and Rhaeadr Mawddach, 2 miles north-east of Ganllwyd, lie in the heart of Coed y Brenin.

Garreg (Llanfrothen) (SH 6141)   A hamlet 2 miles north of Penrhyndeudraeth. Just up the lane north-east towards Croesor is Plas Brondanw where architect Clough Williams Ellis (1883–1978) lived. In the grounds opposite (open to the public) is his folly tower which enjoys wide vistas.

Glan Conwy (SH 8076)   An estuaryside village with much modern housing, 1½ miles south of Llandudno Junction. Nearby is Felin Isaf, a recently restored seventeenth-century watermill grinding flour and open to visitors.

Glyder Fawr (SH 6457) and Glyder Fach (SH 6558)   These twin summits, less than a mile apart and separated only by a shallow saddle, are the highest points of the Glyder range. With their neighbour Tryfan they make a spacious wilderness largely covered by the shattered relics of ancient peaks piled up in strange shapes, especially on Glyder Fach. First, coming from Glyder Fawr, there is Castell y Gwynt (Castle of the Wind) – a jagged ruin of rock with a marvellous view of Snowdon. Then beyond you discover even more striking wrecks. These superb heights are much climbed from Ogwen via Cwm Idwal or Cwm Bochllwyd. Among other paths are those from Capel Curig, Pen-y-gwryd and Pen-y-pass.

Gwydir Castle (SH 7961)   In the Conwy valley across the river from Llanrwst, Gwydir is on a site that was much embattled in the Dark and Middle Ages. The old gateway bears the date 1555 but much of the Elizabethan house has been lost in fires. The house and its grounds are open to the public. There are gardens and fine trees including a huge yew whose age is beyond the telling. Peacocks, some white, strut about or look down at you from the walls.

Gwydir Uchaf chapel (SH 794609)   The chapel is just up the spruce-shaded hill above Gwydir Castle. Built by the Wynn family in the late seventeenth century it is a most interesting edifice, amongst its many unusual features being its ceiling painted with cherubs and angels. There is also much good woodwork – gallery, pews, panelling, pulpit and carved heads.

Gwydyr Forest (SH 7855)   This is a large Forestry Commission plantation centred on Betws-y-coed and the valleys of the Conwy, Llugwy, Lledr and Machno rivers. It was established from 1920 onwards on what was the Gwydir estate of the Wynn family. The original forest was mostly of oak and beech and occupied the valley lands. The bulk of the Forestry Commission plantings have been made on what was a large area of upland sheep country which included lead mines and a few slate quarries, all now defunct. In this long-popular region, every effort has been made to provide public access. There are many nature trails, forest walks, viewpoints and picnic sites of which details are available at Y Stablau, the Park's information centre in the middle of Betws-y-coed.

Harlech (SH 5831)   Sharing the fate of Dinas Mawddwy, in the Middle Ages Harlech had considerable political importance, but not now. Even the sea which used to wash its cliffs is now half a mile beyond the dunes. But it retains a huge symbol of its former glory – Edward I's noble castle, completed in 1289. It was taken by the Welsh under Glyndwr and held by them for several years. Harlech

The marsh helleborine, flowering mid-July to mid-August, grows in the dunes at Morfa Harlech and Morfa Dyffryn in damp areas where the sand is lime-rich with fragments of marine shells

The remains of Iron Age houses and their fields can be seen at Muriau'r Gwyddelod ('Irishmen's Walls') above Harlech. The whole district is rich in prehistory

has other attractions besides this high-perched castle: miles of sandy foreshore and, behind the dunes, a national nature reserve. Since 1927 there has been a college here – Coleg Harlech – which provides residential courses for adults. There is a famous golf course, the Royal St Davids. And for walkers there is all the lovely wild Rhinog country rising away inland. In the centre of the town is a Park information centre. Merthyr Farm, on the Llanfair–Talsarnau road 2 miles north-east of Harlech, has a farm trail open to the public.

Llanaber (SH 6017)   As you come clear of the houses of Barmouth on the Harlech road you have the church of Llanaber looking seawards on your left. This was Barmouth parish church (thirteenth-century) before it was superseded by the present one in the town. As people moved down to live nearer the estuary the original village decayed and Llanaber church was left in isolation. Perhaps this saved it from the worst excesses of Victorian restoration for it is now one of the best medieval survivals in the district.

Llanbedr (SH 5726)   A village on the coast road and railway 3 miles south of Harlech and at the head of the Artro estuary, Llanbedr is a popular resort for yachts. The district has strong Bronze Age links in the form of cairns and standing stones and in the church there is a stone carved with a spiral pattern. Modern artistic aspirations are demonstrated in the Llanbedr craft village (entry charge). In prehistory Llanbedr was a gateway to the Rhinog uplands and so it is today, leading up the delightful Artro to Cwm Bychan and the Roman Steps or up the tributary Nantcol to Rhinog Fawr, Rhinog Fach and Bwlch Drws Ardudwy – all magnificent walking country.

Llanbedr-y-cennin (SH 7569)   This village is 6 miles south of Conwy. 'Cennin' usually means leeks but when linked with St Peter (Pedr or Bedr) cennin are daffodils. This parish has some wild daffodils which, although featured on the Park signs, are generally rare in Snowdonia. Above the village is the hill fort, Pen-y-gaer, unique in north Wales for its defences of upturned stones (*chevaux de frise*) for frustrating cavalry charges.

Llanberis (SH 5760)   At the foot of Snowdon and 7 miles from Caernarfon along A4086, Llanberis has long been a mountaineering centre. Eighteenth-century tourists flocked here even when there was no road at all: they walked or rode from Caernarfon to the north end of Llyn Padarn then got to Llanberis by boat. Tourism took a big step forward with the opening of the Snowdon Mountain Railway.

To appreciate Llanberis and its place in the world you could well begin by visiting Oriel Eryri, the Welsh Environment Gallery near the lake shore. At this out-station of the National Museum of Wales, Cardiff, you will learn all about Snowdonia's history, geography, geology, wildlife, farming, crafts and industries as well as its environmental and conservation problems. There are also art and photography exhibitions. A rock garden dedicated to Edward Lhuyd, pioneer Welsh naturalist, antiquarian and philologist, features many of Snowdon's alpine plants.

Across the lake you see the huge Dinorwig quarries terraced up the slopes of Elidir Fawr. They are not exhausted quarries but closed in 1969 because the demand for slate had slumped. Today the North Wales Quarrying Museum gives you the whole story of the industry. In the adjacent Padarn Country Park you can ride on a narrow-gauge steam railway along the edge of the lake; or you can venture along waterside trails or climb up through oakwoods to see the old quarries.

Among other attractions of Llanberis are the Ceunant Mawr and other falls; boating and angling on the lake; Bryn Bras Castle with extensive grounds open to the public 2 miles towards Caernarfon near A4086; and Dolbadarn Castle, a beautifully sited thirteenth-century round keep overlooking Llyn Peris and probably built by Llywelyn Fawr.

Among the longer walks from Llanberis, apart from the extremely popular track up Snowdon close to the railway, there is one which goes due south over Bwlch Maes-gwm and down to Llyn Cwellyn near the Snowdon Ranger youth hostel.

Llandanwg church (SH 5728)   Mountainous dunes have developed round this little seashore church since it was built in the Middle Ages, perhaps to serve pilgrims on their way across the sea to Bardsey Island. The sand has often nearly buried the church and though strenuous efforts are being made to keep the dunes from advancing much of the churchyard is still engulfed.

Llandegai (SH 5970)   Here next-door to Penrhyn Castle, Bangor, Lord Penrhyn built an estate for his quarry workers and there is modern housing also. Approached along an avenue of venerable yew trees, the cruciform church contains three notable monuments, especially imposing and ornate being that of the first Lord Penrhyn (d 1808).

Llandudno (SH 7782)   Three miles outside the northern boundary of the Park and by far the biggest holiday resort in north Wales, Llandudno is an important base for Park visitors. From its magnificent limestone headland, the Great Orme, reached by tram, cabin lift, road and footpaths, there are splendid views of coast and mountains, especially the Carneddau. A special link with the Park is the museum and art centre, Rapallo House, where you can see finds from the Roman fort at Caerhun. Railway enthusiasts can go by train from Llandudno up the beautiful Lledr valley to Blaenau Ffestiniog and then on the narrow-gauge to Porthmadog, the only way to go right across the Park by rail.

Llanegryn (SH 6005)   A village in the lower Dysynni valley near Tywyn. Up the hill north-west is the medieval church much visited for its carved oak screen, one of the finest surviving in Wales. From Llanegryn footpaths go west to the coast and north to the hills. Nearby there is also Ffordd Ddu, now a mountain track but formerly the main link between Tywyn and Dolgellau. It goes over the western end of the Cader Idris range.

Llanelltyd (SH 7119)   A village on A470 2 miles north-west of Dolgellau, marred by a hideous excess of lamp standards. The medieval church is interesting and made attractive by the well-displayed information about its history. Close by stood Cymer Abbey whose church walls still survive rather picturesquely though so incompletely. Up Cwm yr Wnin to the north you can walk 2 miles to the top of Y Garn but if you are less energetic you can turn left after a mile and follow New Precipice Walk and enjoy marvellous views of Cader Idris and the estuary, coming down after 2 miles to the main road opposite Penmaenpool.

Llanfachreth (SH 7522)   This is an enviably withdrawn, semi-upland village 3 miles north-east of Dolgellau, facing the sun and sheltered from the north by mountains. Prominent in its view is Foel (or Moel) Offrwm which has an Iron Age fort on the top and grand prospects of Cader Idris. The great estate hereabouts was Nannau, a house of some history. You can pick out its houses and cottages by their decorated chimneys. Roads and tracks go off in all directions from the village, some exploring the nearby forest of Coed y Brenin. The challenge for hill walkers is the ascent of Rhobell Fawr, a fine rock-strewn summit 3 miles north-east. A mile west of the village the Forestry Commission has a collection of unusual trees.

Llanfairfechan (SH 6774)   A small seaside holiday town immediately west of Penmaenmawr Mountain, much of Llanfairfechan is tucked into the shelter of a narrow wooded valley. It has wide bathing sands, sailing and angling, and its unspoilt nineteenth-century seafront looks north across the water to Anglesey and the Great Orme. There are walks inland to the local hills and a History Trail which does a round of hut circles, standing stones, a burial chamber and a Roman road. You can set off on greater adventures to the summits of the high Carneddau.

Llanfihangel-y-pennant (SH 6708)   Situated at the western approaches to Cader Idris, this hamlet is well known for its memorial to brave Mary Jones who in 1800, aged sixteen, went barefoot and alone to Bala and back (50 miles) to obtain a Bible from the great preacher Thomas Charles who was inspired by her example to launch the British and Foreign Bible Society. Her grave is at Bryncrug; her Bible is preserved at the society's headquarters in London. The path up to Cader Idris from here was originally a pony track over to Dolgellau. At the watershed you turn along the Cyfrwy ('the saddle') and follow the ridge to the summit. Close to Llanfihangel are the remains of the medieval stronghold, Castell y Bere.

Llangelynnin church near Tywyn (SH 571072)   Two miles down the coast from Llwyngwril, this primitive twelfth-century building has the sea almost immediately below it. Inside is a rare horse-bier and nineteenth-century pews with names painted on them.

Llangelynnin old church near Conwy (SH 751737)   You meander far and high up the lanes to find this simple moorland church 3 miles south-west of Conwy. It dates from thirteenth to sixteenth century and has a wonderfully ancient atmosphere.

Llanrwst (SH 8061)   A gateway to the Park in the north-east, Llanrwst is a small lively market town and tourist centre on the Conwy 5 miles downstream from Betws-y-coed. Apart from its beautiful valley setting and its view to the Carneddau, its main attractions are its bridge and its church. The renowned London architect Inigo Jones (1573–1652) is always supposed to have designed the three-arched bridge over the river but there is no real evidence for this. No matter, it is by popular consent the most elegant stone bridge in north Wales and it has the Stuart arms and the date 1636 carved above the central arch on the upstream side. At the end of the bridge is Llanrwst's oldest house, a charming seventeenth-century National Trust cottage, now a café, called Tu-hwnt-i'r Bont ('beyond the bridge'). In the much restored church a medieval wooden screen survives, intricately carved with vine leaves and grapes, birds pecking at fruit and pigs rooting for acorns. Added to the church in 1634, the family chapel of the Wynns of nearby Gwydir Castle contains many family memorials in marble and brass. There is a medieval knight in effigy and, most impressive, a massive stone tomb doubtfully claimed to be that of Llywelyn the Great who was buried at Aberconwy Abbey in 1240. It is said that the tomb was moved, with the abbey, from Conwy to Maenan in 1283, then to Llanrwst church at the Dissolution (1530s), finally into the Gwydir chapel in the seventeenth century, as a contemporary brass plate informs us.

Llanuwchllyn (SH 8729)   A village near the opposite end of the lake from Bala, Llanuwchllyn is a starting point for walks on the Aran range. There are motorable but very narrow lanes to Dinas Mawddwy up the Twrch valley and to Trawsfynydd up the Lliw valley. The Roman fort, Caer Gai, is one mile north. A medieval

176

fortress, Castell Carn Dochan, 2 miles west, is a place of little history: possibly the fourteenth-century knight whose effigy lies in the church was connected with it. On the main road near the village two statues stand side by side: they are of Sir Owen M. Edwards, a distinguished Welsh educationalist, and his son, Sir Ifan, founder of Urdd Gobaith Cymru (the Welsh League of Youth). The nearby lake-edge estate of Glanllyn is a centre for Urdd activities. Llanuwchllyn is the head-quarters of the lakeside narrow-gauge railway which operates along a short section of the former standard-gauge line from Ruabon to Barmouth.

Llanycil church (SH 9134)   The old parish church of Bala stands at the lakeside in one of the most beautifully situated churchyards in Wales. Here is buried the Rev Thomas Charles (1755–1814), pioneer of Methodism, and the church contains interesting memorials.

Llwyngwril (SH 5909)   This is a large seaside village with extensive caravan sites. Its original parish church, long superseded, survives on the cliffs 2 miles south (see **Llangelynnin**). Another antiquity is the very early Quaker burial ground in the village. Dated 1646 it is a reminder of the days before 1688 when religious persecution drove Quakers to seek refuge in these remote parts. A local viewpoint is Castell-y-gaer, an Iron Age fort above the village. From there by lane and path you can go on 2 miles south to Llanegryn.

Llyn Penmaen (Penmaenpool) (SH 6918)   This is a village on A493 with an attractive old waterside inn on the south bank of the Mawddach estuary. Here, 2 miles west of Dolgellau, a toll bridge provides the lowest vehicular crossing of the tidal river. Since the closing of the railway, the station and signal box have been converted into an excellent Nature Information Centre with estuary birdwatching. The old line is now a public footpath which takes you 5 miles down to the coast with lovely views of the hills and glimpses of the estuary.

Machynlleth (SH 7400)   A small tourist and market town at an ancient crossing of the Dyfi (famous for salmon and sea trout), Machynlleth is the southern entrance to the Park. The attractive, five-arched, stone bridge is centuries old. The town still keeps its wide Norman main street in which an official Wednesday market has been held since 1291. By following the interesting town trail devised by the Civic Society you will see all the buildings of historic value. The ornate Victorian clock tower in the town centre is irresistible to photographers. Three miles north along A487 in a disused quarry is the Centre for Alternative Technology whose message to the world is that we should conserve our natural resources by using wind, water and sun much more than we do at present.

Mallwyd (SH 8612)   A small village at the road junction 1½ miles south of Dinas Mawddwy. The name Brigands' Inn records the wild bandits who terrorised this district in the sixteenth century. The church looks very odd with its seventeenth-century plank tower (and Latin lettering on it) and the rib and vertebra, over the porch, of a prehistoric ox (aurochs) no doubt dug up in a local peat bog.

Minffordd (SH 5938)   This is a village 2 miles east of Porthmadog with stations on the main coast line and the Ffestiniog Railway. Nearby is Portmeirion, the most un-Welsh village in Wales, an architectural fantasy created by Sir Clough Williams Ellis (1883–1978) who has told its full story in his books. The style is that of a colourful Italian coastal village but parts of various British buildings have been re-erected here also. Portmeirion, which is private (entrance fee payable), slopes to the Dwyryd estuary and looks into the sun. As well as accommodation and a restaurant there are shops selling crafts including the well-known Portmeirion pottery. There are walks through gardens (rhododendrons a speciality) along the shore to the headland.

Mochras (SH 5526)   'Shell Island' is not an island but a peninsula which almost blocks the mouth of the Artro 2 miles west of Llanbedr. It is not accessible by car at high tide. It has long been visited for the variety of shells on the beach. From here St Patrick's Causeway stretches seawards and is best seen at low spring tides. Mochras is private and a parking charge is made.

Moel Hebog (SH 5646)   This is the commanding height you see in the south-west from Beddgelert. It is usually climbed either from Beddgelert or Cwm Pennant. But for a super ridge walk you could first take in Moel Ddu by starting from Pont Aberglaslyn. From the top of Hebog it is an easy descent north down its grassy shoulders before you get involved in the rocks of Moel yr Ogof after which you dip and rise again to Moel Lefn. Then, if time and energy allow, you could go on to Trum y Ddysgl and the other alluring summits which curve round the head of Cwm Pennant.

Moel Siabod (SH 7054)   An isolated summit, Siabod has great mountain views especially of the Snowdon Horseshoe and Glyder. South-west it looks across to Moelwyn and Cnicht. It is usually climbed from Capel Curig either from Plas y Brenin or from Pont Cyfyng (SH 734572).

Moelwyn range (SH 6544)   These hills between Snowdon and Rhinog look especially attractive from Trawsfynydd across the Vale of Ffestiniog. The summits are Moelwyn Mawr, Moelwyn Bach and Moel-yr-hydd. Standing apart in the north-west is Cnicht which looks such a very sharp peak from Porthmadog. An outlier to the east of Moelwyn is the round dome of Manod Mawr. Cnicht is often climbed from the Nantmor valley or Cwm Croesor. Cwmorthin is the natural gateway to the Moelwyn group, but go up from the Stwlan reservoir if you like things the hard way. Manod Mawr can be tackled from Cwm Teigl in the east or Blaenau Ffestiniog in the west.

Mynydd Mawr (SH 5354)   The bold hill seen reflected in the waters of Llyn Cwellyn as you travel along A4085, Mynydd Mawr stands isolated by deep valleys and there are lines of high cliffs north and south. It is usually climbed from Rhyd-ddu.

Nant Ffrancon (SH 6363)   One of Snowdonia's most majestic valleys, Nant Ffrancon's wild beauty is best seen as you go up from Bethesda with the bold shapes of Tryfan, Glyder Fawr and Y Garn high before you, their flanks hollowed by the great corries of Cwm Idwal and its neighbours. No vehicular road came this way until the late eighteenth century (Lord Penrhyn's slate-traffic route). Telford's road had superseded it by 1830.

Nant Gwynant (SH 6250) One of the best-loved valleys in the Park, Nant Gwynant has two perfect lakes, Dinas and Gwynant, lying beneath vast steep slopes which are wooded below, rockier higher up. From the village between the lakes the Watkin Path goes north up Snowdon; and to the south a narrow, twisting, gated lane takes you over a ridge and down the splendid Nantmor valley under the arid rocks of Yr Arddu, an outlier of Cnicht.

Nantlle Valley (SH 5453) Along this valley B4418 takes you 6 miles east from the slate quarries around Pen-y-groes to Rhyd-ddu on A4085. The vast quarries are the special delight of industrial archaeologists; then once you are into the Park by Llyn Nantlle Uchaf you enter a magnificent glen between high, craggy slopes and you have spectacular views of Snowdon as you go up to Drws-y-coed. There is now little to be seen of the big copper mine which operated in this pass until 1920.

Nant Peris (SH 6058) The village has a large car park and is on A4086 at the bottom of Llanberis Pass. Footpaths go from here over the Glyder range and down to Nant Ffrancon. Nant Peris was the original Llanberis before the present one developed as the Dinorwig quarry got busy in the nineteenth century. The parish church, dedicated to the Celtic Saint Peris, keeps some of its medieval features but nineteenth-century restoration was severe. In a field across the road is Ffynnon Beris, a healing and wishing well once famous for miles around. Llyn Peris, the upper of the two Llanberis lakes, has lately been made part of the Dinorwig hydro-electricity project. Above the head of the lake on the slopes of Snowdon are the remains of a copper mine.

Penmachno (SH 7850) Two miles up A5 from the Waterloo Bridge at Betws-y-coed the Machno stream flows into the Conwy in a wooded gorge thunderous with two lovely waterfalls, one on each river. Here you turn right along B4406 and in half a mile you come to a woollen mill where visitors are welcome. It is another 1½ miles to the former slate-quarrying village of Penmachno, long known for the early Christian inscribed stones in the medieval church. Penmachno's five-arched bridge is eighteenth century and the parish abounds with ancient dwellings. One of these is the National Trust cottage, Tŷ Mawr, birthplace of Bishop Morgan who made the first translation of the Bible into Welsh (printed in London in 1588) thus giving an enormous fillip to the language. Tŷ Mawr is reached from Penmachno along a 2 mile road dark with conifers. Another road, which comes up from the Lledr valley, is not recommended for cars.

Penmaenmawr Mountain (SH 7075) All along the north between Aber and Conwy the foothills of the Carneddau come boldly to the coast, especially on the great headland of Penmaenmawr whose slopes, much quarried for road-stone, plunge steeply to the coast road (A55). Until the eighteenth century what was called 'the great Irish road' crept precariously across the seaward face of Penmaenmawr and was a source of terror to travellers. In fact it was impassable to carriages and they had to be dismantled and carried over this difficult place and then re-assembled.

Penmaenmawr town (SH 7176)   This holiday resort just outside the Park on the north coast road (A55) is popular for its sands, bathing, yachting, water skiing and sea angling. Over the sea it looks across to Anglesey, Puffin Island and the Great Orme. Penmaenmawr began as a quarry village and stone is still shipped from its quay. Some of the local walks are decidedly for the energetic, like the one that takes you to the top of the mountain high above the town, or another which goes up to the so-called Druids' Circle, a Bronze Age ring of ten standing stones (SH 723746). The walks up these slopes are featured in an interesting History Trail, a leaflet about which can be obtained in local shops.

Pennal (SH 6900)   This small village is 4 miles from Machynlleth along A493 towards Aberdyfi. Here was a perhaps large Roman fort but traces of it are now very slight and a farmhouse stands on it. This is very much Owain Glyndwr country. From Pennal in 1404, at the height of his rebellion, he wrote a letter (still preserved in Paris) asking the King of France to help in the struggle against the English. An oak-clad castle mound (possibly twelfth century) survives between the village and Talgarth Hall.

Penrhyn Castle (SH 6071)   Two miles east of Bangor this incredible but very photogenic edifice stands in its rolling acres on a historic site though its own history is mainly nineteenth century. Now belonging to the National Trust this pseudo-medieval fortress-residence is the ultimate in delusions of grandeur. The wealth to build it came from Lord Penrhyn's quarries at Bethesda. The outbuildings contain a railway museum and inside, too, the castle is museum-like, crammed with historical, artistic and curious objects including a large collection of the world's dolls. As well as a magnificent hall and staircases, there are splendid dining rooms, library, chapel, bedrooms (William Morris wallpaper) and servants' quarters. Everywhere the plasterwork and the wood and stone carving are of a high order. If you love Victoriana you will be in raptures. If not, you may find it all too ostentatious. But you will enjoy the magnificent trees and shrubs, especially the eucryphias in late summer.

Penrhyndeudraeth (SH 6139)   On A487 3 miles east of Porthmadog, this town-sized village which developed with the nineteenth-century slate industry is at the head of the Dwyryd estuary (Traeth Bach). The offices of the National Park Authority and a Park information centre are here, and there are stations on the Cambrian Coast and the Ffestiniog lines. The Vale of Ffestiniog stretches north-east rising to Moelwyn and Cnicht. Just east of the village, Coed Cae Fali, a National Trust woodland, clothes the hillside in beauty.

Pen-y-gwryd (SH 6555)   The most celebrated hotel in Welsh mountaineering history (opened in 1847) stands in moorland isolation at the junction of A4086 and A498 1 mile east of Pen-y-pass. From here rock-climbing in Snowdonia was pioneered from the 1850s onwards. The hotel is built on the site of a Roman camp whose south-western banks are still clear to see.

Pen-y-pass (SH 6455)   This is the top of Llanberis Pass on A4086. A youth hostel, a restaurant, a Park rangers' post and a car park now occupy the site. Before that there was the Pen-y-pass hotel, a part of which is incorporated into the hostel building. The history of Snowdonian rock-climbing from the start of the twentieth century was bound up with that hotel. A medieval name for Pen-y-pass is Gorffwysfa Peris ('the resting place of St Peris') and no doubt it was kept as a hallowed spot because this Celtic holy man had stayed there awhile on his travels. Today Pen-y-pass is a very popular starting point for Snowdon and Glyder and at times there are severe parking problems.

Port Dinorwig (Dinorwic) (SH 5267)   A small town on the Menai Strait 5 miles south-west of Bangor, Dinorwig was founded just after 1800 to export the slates from Llanberis (brought down by narrow-gauge line from 1825 onwards). It is now largely residential and has a marina. From here the Romans are thought to have crossed the strait in their invasions of Anglesey in AD61 and 78.

Porthmadog (SH 5738)   A busy little port for nineteenth-century coastal trading; boats were built at Porthmadog and much Ffestiniog slate exported. It is now a yachting centre and, with Borth y Gest and Morfa Bychan, a popular holiday resort well placed for exploring western Snowdonia. It is on the main coast line and is the headquarters of the Ffestiniog Railway (with museum). At the harbour is a maritime museum complete with sailing ship. You can try throwing your own pots at Porthmadog Pottery. The nearby Traeth Mawr was a beautiful estuary until it was destroyed by the ugly wall (the Cob) in 1811. The poet Shelley, who ought to have known better, called it 'one of the noblest works of human power'.

Rhinog (SH 6528)   From east or west this undulating range stretching 14 miles from Maentwrog to Barmouth makes an exciting skyline. The summit nearest to Barmouth is Diffwys which is partly grassy, partly rocky with east-facing cliffs. Its neighbour is Y Llethr, the highest of the whole range, and there is an outlier, Y Garn, near Dolgellau. Further north the going gets ever more rocky and Rhinog Fach, then Rhinog Fawr, are truly craggy. The northern end of these hills, rising to Moel Ysgyfarnogod, is a wilderness of bare rock, scree and heather. There are two high passes, Bwlch Drws Ardudwy and Bwlch Tyddiad (which has the Roman Steps); and there are many small lakes in wild surroundings. Prehistoric remains are many. From the recent past there are deserted mines, especially manganese, and there are slate caverns at Llanfair.

Rhosgadfan (SH 5057)   Just outside the Park, 4 miles south-east of Caernarfon, this is one of many similar villages of the Nantlle slate region. Here is preserved Cae'r Gors, a roofless cottage: it is the humble birthplace of Kate Roberts (1891–1985), distinguished writer of novels and short stories in Welsh. A nearby village is Rhostryfan where an eighteenth-century slate-worker's cottage was removed and rebuilt at St Fagan's folk museum, Cardiff.

Rhyd-ddu (SH 5652)   A village on A4085, 4 miles north-west of Beddgelert, Rhyd-ddu is a good starting place for walks up Snowdon, Mynydd Mawr, the

Nantlle hills and to two fair waters, Llyn y Dywarchen and Llyn y Gader.

Roman Steps (SH 6530)   Almost certainly not Roman, these hundreds of steps climbing through rocks and heather up the west side of the Rhinog range may have originated as part of a late medieval or more recent trade route between the Harlech region and England. Or possibly they go right back to the time of Harlech Castle and were a link in a political and military road between Harlech, Bala and London.

Ro-wen (SH 7571)   One of the Park's best-kept villages, Ro-wen is sequestered along the lanes 5 miles south of Conwy under the slopes of the Carneddau foot-hills. Among the many enjoyable hill walks are those over Tal y Fan or through the gap of Bwlch y Ddeufaen.

Sarn Helen   On some maps this Roman road strides boldly down the Park from north to south but when you come to look for it on the ground you soon find your-self hesitant, nonplussed or downright defeated, perhaps up to your knees in bogs that stretch far and wide.

Snowdon (SH 6054)   The English name was originally Snaudun (snau = snow, dun = hill) and on clear winter days its gleaming white peak is visible from vast distances. In Welsh it is Yr Wyddfa 'the tumulus', a name connected with the legend of a giant buried under the original summit cairn which was presumably of the Bronze Age.

On a fine summer's day you may have to share the top of Britain's most popular mountain with a thousand others. Even if you go by night to see the sunrise you may not have it to yourself – for two hundred years people have gone up by star-light or moonlight, especially this century when large parties of Welsh lads and lasses have walked up from Llanberis at harvest moon, some gathering from as far away as Liverpool. Among other ascents are those by athletes who race to the top and back, or include Snowdon along with a dash up Scafell Pike and Ben Nevis all in one day. In the nineteenth century a guide from Llanberis went up Snowdon 2,000 times. In the twentieth century a Beddgelert artist managed it 560 times. And from Rhyd-ddu a man of fifty-six got to the top three times in one day.

Snowdon Mountain Railway   The heavy thumping of the Snowdon railway engines is an accepted part of the summer scene. It can be heard in every corrie and on every ridge as well as from mountains miles away. Britain's only cog railway has been steaming people up from Llanberis since 1896. Its seven Swiss-made, coal-burning engines each push one coach up at nearly 5mph and take one hour up and one down, climbing over 3,000ft (915m) in 4½ miles. There is a single track (gauge 2ft 7½in) with passing places. The service lasts from Easter to early October and summit refreshments are available whenever the trains are running.

Snowdon Sherpa service   This very useful summer bus service around Snowdon is not only a spectacular scenic journey, it is also a great help to hill walkers, freeing them from having to retrace their steps to their cars. Parking in Llanberis Pass can be so difficult it is often best to leave your car at Nant Peris car park, take the bus to Pen-y-pass and walk from there.

Swallow Falls (Rhaeadr Ewynnol) (SH 7657)   These falls on A5, 2 miles north-west of Betws-y-coed, are one of the most popular tourist attractions in Wales. There is a vast free car park but you pay to see the falls. 'Swallow' is a mistranslation of *Ewynnol* which really means foaming.

Sygun copper mine (SH 6048)   The mine is 1 mile east of Beddgelert and is open to the public.

Talybont (SH 5921)   A village on the coast road, 4 miles north of Barmouth, Talybont has a most interesting Old Country Life Museum all about earlier farming days and local shipwrecks.

Talyllyn Lake (SH 7109)   Seen from the south-west this lake lies beautifully in the view towards Talyllyn Pass with the high crags of Cader Idris on the left and those of Craig y Llam on the right. The outlines of trout carved on the wall outside the Ty'n-y-cornel hotel show what fine fish inhabit this fertile water. The simple old parish church by the lake's outlet stream has an unusual chancel ceiling of squared panels carved with roses (early seventeenth century).

Tan-y-bwlch, Plas (SH 6540)   This mansion, built in 1748 but much altered, looks across the Vale of Ffestiniog to the village of Maentwrog. It was the home of the Oakeley family, owners of local slate mines. The house and its extensive grounds are now the Park's residential study centre where courses are available on many aspects of the Snowdonia environment. The mature gardens have fine specimen trees and shrubs, including huge old rhododendrons, and there are camellias, magnolias and many other choice plants. There are nature trails through the grounds; and close by are the Ffestiniog narrow-gauge railway and the Coedydd Maentwrog national nature reserve.

Trawsfynydd (SH 7035)   A sizeable moorland village by-passed by A470 11 miles north of Dolgellau. Formerly busy with slate-quarrying (and some fruitless prospecting for gold) it has become well-known this century, first through the creation of its large hydro-electric reservoir (1930), then by the erection of Britain's first inland nuclear power-station (1964), a highly controversial intrusion into the heart of a National Park. The reservoir is popular with anglers (brown trout, rainbows, perch, rudd and grass carp); and for birdwatchers there are in summer many nesting gulls (sometimes terns), oystercatchers and common sandpipers, and in winter rafts of ducks with occasional grebes and wild swans. In the village there is a statue to a young shepherd poet, Hedd Wynn, who did not live to know that he had won the bardic chair at the National Eisteddfod of 1917. He had been killed on the Western Front a few weeks earlier.

Trefriw (SH 7863)   An estuaryside village, formerly a popular spa, on B5106 9 miles south of Conwy. There is a large woollen mill (and shop) where hydro-electric machinery is also on view. One and a half miles south up a steep lane through conifers, is the simple, ancient church of Llanrhychwyn, a lonely building full of the atmosphere of past centuries.

The national nature reserve at Coed Tremadog is on dolerite cliffs and screes that contain enough lime to allow the development of an ashwood and calcicole wildflowers and ferns

Tremadog (SH 5640)   Here, 1 mile north-west of Porthmadog, is a curiosity: a nineteenth-century planned town which never grew up. It was the brain-child of W. A. Madocks, creator of the Porthmadog embankment. Here he built a town hall and square, a few houses, a hotel, a church and a chapel, and they remain as charming relics of the early 1800s. Tremadog was going to be an important place on the road from London to Porth Dinllaen (near Nefyn) which was to be developed as the port for crossing to Ireland. But Holyhead was chosen instead. A plaque on a house in Tremadog indicates the birthplace of Lawrence of Arabia (1888–1935).

Tywyn (SH 5800)   On the coast near the southern tip of the Park, Tywyn is a holiday resort with a long sandy shore and a spacious promenade. The old part of the town lies well back from the sea front, the earliest building being the cruciform parish church which has a twelfth-century nave and is dedicated to the sixth-century Celtic saint, Cadfan, who is reputed to have sailed from here across to Bardsey Island to found a Christian settlement there. A Dark Ages stone in the church is inscribed with the earliest known words of written Welsh, but sadly their meaning is obscure. These days many people come to Tywyn for a trip on the Talyllyn Railway.

Storm waves scouring the sands here occasionally expose the stumps of pre-historic trees, a reminder of the wide lands lost under the sea about five thousand years ago. To explain these forest remains the medieval story-tellers invented the tale of Cantref y Gwaelod, 'the lowland hundred villages' which were inundated for ever when a drunken watchman forgot to close the sea gates. According to the legend the church bells at nearby Aberdyfi can still be heard ringing under the sea when gales are blowing.

Ysbyty Ifan (SH 8448) In the bandit-infested days of the Middle Ages, the Order of St John of Jerusalem established a chain of hospices in western Europe to shelter pilgrims and other travellers. One of their few hospices in Wales was here, perhaps because this part of the Conwy valley was on a pilgrims' route to the very holy island of Bardsey. No trace of the hospice is now visible but it is believed to have stood close to the west side of the present church. This is nineteenth century but contains three recumbent medieval effigies and fragments of carved stones from an earlier church on the site.

APPENDIX 1
PLACE-NAME ELEMENTS

Some place-names are obscure either because their meaning has been forgotten or because they have become distorted from the original form. But most are made up of well-known elements, some of which are listed below while many more will be found in dictionaries. Unless you are Welsh-speaking a name like Rhwngddwyafon may look formidable but when separated into its three parts, *rhwng-ddwy-afon*, it simply means 'between two rivers'. A few places are named after people, legendary or historical: Cewydd, Dafydd, Emrys, Garmon, Gelert, Hywel, Idris, Idwal, Ifan, Llywelyn, Wilym and so on. Many churches and villages remember saints: Capel Curig (St Curig), Llanbedr (St Peter), Llanberis (St Peris), Llandegai (St Tegai), Llandudno (St Tudno), Llanfair (St Mary), Llanfihangel (St Michael), Llanrwst (St Grwst), Llansanffraid (St Bridget). And there are all those communities named after their chapels: Bethesda, Bethel, Carmel and others straight from Palestine.

aber, mouth, confluence
aderyn (pl *adar*), bird
adwy, gap
ael, brow
afon, river, stream
allt, hillside
annedd, dwelling
ar, upon
aran, mountain
ardd, garden
arth, hill

bach, small
bala, outlet of lake
ban (pl *hannau*), summit
banc, hill
bedd (pl *beddau*), grave
bedwen (pl *bedw*), birch
benglog, skull
bera, pyramid
bere, kite, buzzard
berfedd, middle
berllan, orchard
betws, oratory

beudy, cowshed
big, peak
blaen (pl *blaenau*), head of valley
boch, cheek
bod, dwelling
boeth, warm
bont, bridge
braich, arm
bran, crow
bras, prominent
brith, speckled, pied, variegated
bro, region, vale
bron, rounded hill
brwynog, rushy
bryn, hill
buarth, cattle-fold
bwlch, pass
bychan, small
byr, short

cader (*cadair*), chair, fortress
cae, field
caer, fort
cafn, trough

cain, beautiful
cam, crooked
can (cant), a hundred
canol, middle
capel, chapel
carn, carnedd (pl carneddau), heap of
    stones, cairn, mountain
carreg, rock
caseg, mare
castell, castle
cefn, ridge
ceiri, giants
celli, grove
celyn, holly
cemais, bend in river
cennin, leeks
cennin Pedr, daffodils
cerrig, rocks
ceunant, ravine
cidwm, wolf
cigfran, raven
cil (pl ciliau), nook
clafdy, hospital
clawdd (pl cloddiau), embankment
clegyr, crag
clogwyn, cliff
clyd, sheltered
cob, embankment
coch, red
coed, woodland
congl, corner
copa, summit
corlan, sheep-fold
corn, horn
cornel, corner
cors, bog
craf, wild garlic, ramsons
craig (pl creigiau), rock
crib (pl cribau), ridge
cribin, serrated ridge
croes, cross
crug (pl crugiau), mound
cul, narrow
cwm, valley, corrie
cwn, hounds
cwrt, court
cyfrwy, saddle
cyfyng, narrow

cymer, confluence
cyrn, peak
cytiau, huts
cywarch, hemp

dan, under
darren, hill
ddôl, meadow
ddu, black
ddŵr, water
ddysgl, dish
deg, beautiful
derwen (pl derw), oak
deu, two
deulyn, two lakes
diffwys, precipice
din (dinas), fort
diniewyd, bullocks
dir, land
dôl, meadow
domen, mound
draeth, beach
draws, across
dref, hamlet; home
drum, ridge
drws, pass
du (pl duon), black
dulas, dark stream
dwfr (dwr), water
dwy, two
dyffryn, valley
dywarchen, turf

efail, smithy
eglwys, church
eira, snow
eithin, gorse
elen (elain), young deer
elor, bier
erw, acre
eryr, eagle
esgair, ridge
esgob, bishop

fach, small
fan, place, high place
fawn, peat
fawnog, peaty

fawr, large
fechan, small
fedwen (pl *fedw*), birch
felin, mill
ffin, boundary
ffordd, road
ffos, ditch
ffridd (*ffrith*), hillside pasture
ffrwd, waterfall
ffynnon, spring, well
figyn (*fign*), bog
filiast, greyhound
foel, bare hill
fraith, speckled, pied, variegated
fran, crow
fras, prominent
fron, rounded hill
fynach, monk
fynydd, mountain

gader (*gadair*), chair, fortress
gaer, fort
gafr, goat
gallt, hillside
gam, crooked
gardd, garden
garn, rock
garrog, torrent
garth, hill
garw, rough
gath, cat
geifr, goats
gelli, grove
gesail, hollow
gigfran, raven
gil, nook
glan, bank
glas (pl *gleision*), green, blue
glyder, heap
glyn, glen
goch, red
goetre, woodland house
gopa, summit
gors, bog
grach, scabby
graeanog, gravelly
graig, rock
griafolen, rowan tree

gribin, serrated ridge
grisiau, steps
groes, cross
grug, heather
gwair, hay
gwastad, level place
gwaun, moor
gwen, white
gwern, marsh
gwernen, alder
gwŷdd, woodland
Gwyddelod, Irishmen
gwyn, white
gwynt, wind
gyrn, peak

hafod (*hafoty*), summer dwelling
haul, sun
hebog, falcon
heli, salt water
hen, old
hendre, winter dwelling
heol, road
heulog, sunny
hir (pl *hirion*), long
hydd, stag
hyfryd, pleasant
hyll, ugly

isaf, lowest

lan, bank
las, green, blue
lefn, smooth
llam, leap
llan, church, village
llanerch, glade
llawr, flat valley bottom
llech, slate
llechog, slaty
llechwedd, hillside
llefn, smooth
llethr, slope
llety, shelter, lodging
llidiart, gate
llithrig, slippery
lloer, moon
lluest, hut, summer dwelling

llwyd, grey
llwyn, grove
llwynog, fox
llyfn, smooth
llyn (pl *llynnoedd* or *llynnau*), lake
llys, court
lydan, wide

maen, stone
maes, field
maesglasau, field of the green
   mountain(?)
man, high place
march, stallion
marian, shore
mawn, peat
mawnog, peaty
mawr, large
meillionen, clover
meini, stones
meirch, stallions
melin, mill
melyn, yellow
migneint, boggy hollows
migyn (*mign*), bog
min, edge
moch, pigs
moel, bare hill
môr, sea
morfa, coastal marsh
morwynion (*morynion*), maidens
mur (pl *muriau*), wall
mwyn, mineral, ore
mynach, monk
mynydd, mountain

nadroedd, snakes
nant, stream, valley
neuadd, hall
newydd, new

ochr, side
odyn, kiln
oer, cold
ogof (*ogo*), cave
ole (*olau*), light
onnen (pl *onn*), ash tree

pair, cauldron
pandy, fulling mill
pant, hollow
parc, field, park
pen, top
penmaen, rocky promontory
pennant, head of a glen
penrhyn, headland
pentref (*pentre*), village
perfedd, middle
person, parson
pig, peak
pistyll, waterfall
plas, mansion
poeth, warm
pont, bridge
pren, timber
pwll, pit, pool

'r, the, of the
rhaeadr, waterfall
rhedyn, bracken
rhiw, hill
rhos, marsh, moor
rhosdir, moorland
rhudd, red
rhwng, between
rhyd, ford

saeth (pl *saethau*), arrow
sarn, road, especially a paved road
sych, dry

tai, houses
tair, three
tal, end
tan, under
tap, ridge
tarren, hill
teg, beautiful
teyrn, king
tir, land
tomen, mound
traeth, shore
traws, across
tref, hamlet, home
tri, three
troed, foot

tros, over
trum, ridge
trwyn, promontory
twll, hole
twmp, *twmpath*, mound
twr, tower
tŷ, house
tyddyn, smallholding
tywyn, seashore

uchaf, highest
uwch, above

waun (*waen*), moor

wen, white
wrach, witch
wyddfa, burial mound, viewpoint
wyn, white

y, the, of the
yn, in
ynys, island, riverside meadow
yr, the, of the
ysbyty, hospice
ysgol (pl *ysgolion*), ladder, school
ysgubor, barn
ystrad, valley floor
ystum, bend in river

APPENDIX 2
USEFUL ADDRESSES

Cambrian Ornithological Society, 21 Benarth Court, Glan Conwy, Colwyn Bay, Clwyd, LL28 5ED.

Council for National Parks, 45 Shelton Street, London, WC2H 9HJ. This is an independent, voluntary body working for National Park objectives. It organises a supporting group called the Friends of the National Parks.

Council for the Protection of Rural Wales, 31 High Street, Welshpool, Powys, SY21 7JP.

Countryside Commission (Wales Office), 8 Broad Street, Newtown, Powys.

Farm Visits. For details of farms open to the public (trails, educational groups, etc) enquire at the Park information centres, or at the National Park office, Penrhyndeudraeth.

Forestry Commission (Wales Office), Victoria Terrace, Aberystwyth, Dyfed.

National Trust (Wales Office), Trinity Square, Llandudno, Gwynedd, LL30 2DE.

Nature Conservancy Council, Ffordd Penrhos, Bangor, Gwynedd, LL57 2LQ.

North Wales Naturalists' Trust, 376 High Street, Bangor, Gwynedd, LL57 1NU.

Royal Society for the Protection of Birds (Wales Office), Frolic Street, Newtown, Powys, SY16 1AP.

Snowdonia National Park Authority, National Park Office, Penrhyndeudraeth, Gwynedd, LL48 6LS.

Snowdonia National Park Society, Dyffryn Mymbyr, Capel Curig, Betws-y-coed, Gwynedd.

BIBLIOGRAPHY AND MAPS

Allen, P. M. and Jackson, A. A. *Geological Excursions in the Harlech Dome* (British Geological Survey, 1985)

Baughan, P. E. *A Regional History of the Railways of Great Britain (Vol XI) North and Mid Wales* (David & Charles, 1980). A very thorough, detailed account

Benoit, P. and Richards, M. *A Contribution to a Flora of Merioneth* (West Wales Naturalists' Trust, 1963)

Bick, D. E. *The Old Copper Mines of Snowdonia* (Pound House, 1982). Industrial archaeology in meticulous detail

Bowen, E. G. and Gresham, C. *The History of Merioneth, (Vol 1)* (Merioneth Historical and Record Society, 1967). An erudite survey of the region's prehistoric monuments

Boyd, J. I. C., *The Ffestiniog Railway* (Oakwood Press, 1975). The authoritative history in two volumes

Carr, H. R. C. and Lister, G. A. *The Mountains of Snowdonia* (Lane, 2nd. ed. 1948). Very informative on a wide range of subjects: geology, topography, natural history, climbing, etc

Challinor, J. and Bates, D. *Geology Explained in North Wales* (David & Charles, 1973)

Clark, R. W. and Pyatt, E. C. *Mountaineering in Britain* (Phoenix House, 1957). Includes a very good account of the history of climbing in Snowdonia

Condry, W. *The Snowdonia National Park* (Collins, 1966)

Condry, W. *Exploring Wales* (Faber & Faber, 1970)

Condry, W. *Pathway to the Wild* (Faber & Faber, 1975)

Condry, W. *The Natural History of Wales* (Collins, 1981)

Dodd, A. H. *The Industrial Revolution in North Wales* (U. of Wales Press, 1971)

Ellis, R. G. *Flowering Plants of Wales* (National Museum of Wales, 1983). Gives the status and a distribution map of all species

Evans, D. E. *Snowdonia National Park Scenery* (National Museum of Wales, 1977). A booklet of colour photographs with clear explanatory captions about landforms and geology

Forrest, H. E. *The Vertebrate Fauna of North Wales* (Witherby, 1907). A scholarly work of great interest and historical value

George, T. N. *British Regional Geology: North Wales* (HMSO, 1961). A new edition is in preparation

Green, C. C. *Cambrian Railways Album* (Ian Allan, 1977). A fascinating collection of archive photographs

Hall, G. W. *The Gold Mines of Merioneth* (Griffin Publications, 1975)

Houlder, C. *Wales: An Archaeological Guide* (Faber & Faber, 1974)

Howe, G. M. and Thomas, P. *Welsh Landforms and Scenery* (MacMillan, 1965)

Howells, M. F. et al. *Dolgarrog* (HMSO, 1981). A geological guide to the lower Conwy region

Howells, M. F., Leveridge, B. E., and Reedman, A. J. *Snowdonia. A Geological Field Guide* (Unwin Paperbacks, 1981)

Hyde, H. A. and Wade, A. E. *Welsh Ferns* (National Museum of Wales, 1978)

Johnson, P. *The Cambrian Lines* (Ian Allan, 1984). Numerous railway photographs with informative captions

Jones, E. B. and Thomas, G. E. *Birdwatching in Snowdonia* (John Jones, 1976). A very helpful field guide for all seasons

Jones, P. H. *Birds of Merioneth* (Cambrian Ornith. Soc., 1974)

Jones, P. H. and Dare, P. *Birds of Caernarvonshire* (Cambrian Ornith. Soc., 1976)

Lewis, W. J. *Lead-mining in Wales* (University of Wales Press, 1967)

Millward, R. and Robinson, A. *Landscapes of North Wales* (David & Charles, 1978)

Nash-Williams, V. E. *The Roman Frontier in Wales* (University of Wales Press 2nd ed, 1969)

National Trust. *Properties of the National Trust.* An invaluable list which is regularly brought up to date

North, F. J. *The Slates of Wales* (University of Wales Press, 1925)

North, F. J., Campbell, B. and Scott, R. *Snowdonia* (Collins, 1949). F. J. North's summary of the Park's geology, though somewhat dated, is still a classic of popular writing on the subject

North, F. J. *Mining for Metals in Wales* (National Museum of Wales, 1962)

Poucher, W. A. *The Welsh Peaks* (Constable, eighth edition, 1983)

Rees, D. M. *Mines, Mills and Furnaces* (National Museum of Wales, 1969)

Roberts, B. *The Geology of Snowdonia and Llŷn. A Field Guide* (Adam Hilger, 1979)

Royal Commission on Ancient Monuments *Caernarvonshire* (3 vols) (HMSO, 1956–64)

Royal Commission on Ancient Monuments *Merionethshire* (HMSO, 1921)

Styles, S. *The Mountains of North Wales* (Gollancz, 1973)

Turner, K. *The Snowdon Mountain Railway* (David & Charles, 1973)

Watson, K. *Regional Archaeologies: North Wales* (Cory, Adams and Mackay, 1965)

Young, G. W., Sutton, G. and Noyce, W. *Snowdon Biography* (J. M. Dent, 1957). Entertaining rock-climbers' reminiscences

Maps

OS Landranger Series 1:50 000, sheets 115, 116, 124, 125, 135

OS Outdoor Leisure Maps 1:25 000, sheets 16, 17, 18, 19, 23

West Col Mountain Maps 1:25 000
    Northern Sheet – Glyders and Carneddau
    Southern Sheet – Snowdon and Glyders

Geology maps: besides the small-scale maps (eg the quarter-inch) covering the solid geology of north Wales there is an invaluable 1:25 000 sheet (1972) entitled *Central Snowdonia* in the 'Classical Areas of British Geology' series of the British Geological Survey

INDEX

Many place names will be found under the following headings: mountains under Mynydd, Moel or Foel; lakes under Llyn; valleys and corries under Cwm; bridges under Pont; passes under Bwlch; woodlands under Coed; and waterfalls under Rhaeadr.

Canovium, 97, 161
Cantref y Gwaelod, 184–5
Capel Celyn, 126
Capel Curig, 121, 123, 140, 145, 147, 162–3
Capel Garmon, 92, 121, 163
Capel Hermon, 114
Caraway, whorled, 54
Carneddau Hengwm, 92, 163–4
Carneddau range, 22, 26, 142–4, 163–4
Carnedd Dafydd, 42, 143, 160, 164
Carnedd-goch, 146
Carnedd Llywelyn, 60, 143, 144, 160, 164
Carnedd y Filiast (Glyder), 26, 142; (Nr Bala), 126, 150
Carp, grass, 70
Carrot, 56
Castell Carndochan, 116, 151, 177
Castell Prysor, 164
Castell y Bere, 100, 128
Cat's-ear, smooth, 88
Cefn-caer, 97
Celandine, lesser, 53
Centaury, 87
Cerrigydrudion, 126
Ceunant Llennyrch, 124, 149
Chaffinch, 64
Char, 69–70
Chickweed, alpine, 46; arctic, 46
Chough, 59, 77, 84
Churchyards, 55
Cinquefoil, alpine, 47; marsh, 50, 76
Cleavage, 36
Clogwyn Du'r Arddu, 42, 44, 77, 137
Clogwyn y Garnedd, 77, 137
Clubmosses, 44
Cnicht, 32, 123, 147, 148, 166, 178
Cochwillan, 160
Coed Camlyn, 81
Coed Cymerau, 80–1
Coed Dolgarrog, 82–3
Coed Ganllwyd, 80
Coed Gorswen, 83
Coed Tremadog, 84, 184
Coed y Brenin, 20, 66, 127, 151, 164, 171
Coedydd Aber, 83–4
Coedydd Maentwrog, 81, 123, 135
Coed y Rhygen, 82
Conifer plantations, 19, 63–4, 126, 127, 151, 154, 155
Conwy, 102, 120, 128, 161, 164; abbey, 100; castle, 100, 164; Mountain, 96, 143, 164; river, 124, 125; suspension bridge, 117; tubular bridge, 117–8; valley, 120–1
Coot, 62
Copper mines, 107, 112–4, 167, 179
Cord-grass, 56
Cormorant, 59, 76
Corries, 39, 77, 79
Corris, 128, 155, 165; railway, 128, 129, 135–6; quarries, 109, 111, 165
Cors Fochno, 89
Cotton grass, 50
Cow-wheat, 53
Craig Cwm Silyn, 146
Craig Maesglasau, 153
Craig Portas, 153

Craig y Bera, 145
Craig y Dinas, 96
Craig y Llam, 153
Craig yr Aderyn, 35, 65, 96, 165, 166
Craig-yr-ysfa, 37, 143, 144
Crane's-bill, shining, 83, 84
Creeper, tree, 64
Cregennen Lakes, 87, 94, 154, 157
Creigiau Gleision, 78, 145
Crib Goch, 35, 42, 139, 166
Crib y Ddysgl, 138, 139, 166
Cricieth (or Criccieth), 96, 147; castle, 100
Crimea Pass, 169
Croesor, 148, 166
Cross Foxes, 127, 153
Crossbill, 64
Crow, carrion, 60, 64
Crowfoot, water, 53
Curlew, 62, 64, 65
Cwm Bochlwyd, 140
Cwm Bual, 142
Cwm Bychan, Llanbedr, 149, 166; Nantmor, 166
Cwm Cau, 32, 39, 80
Cwm Cewydd, 153
Cwm Ciprwth, 146
Cwm Clyd, 140
Cwm Clywedog, 153–4
Cwm Cywarch, 39, 152
Cwm Dulyn, 146
Cwm Dyli, 166
Cwm Einion, 171
Cwm Geu Graig, 127
Cwm Glas Crafnant, 77–8, 78
Cwm Glas-mawr, 43, 123
Cwm Hirnant, 126, 154
Cwm Idwal, 9, 37, 39, 43, 76, 121, 166–7; nature reserve, 74–7
Cwm Llefrith, 147
Cwm Maethlon, 128, 131, 155
Cwm Moch, 81, 94, 96–7
Cwm Mynach, 116, 152
Cwmorthin, 148
Cwm Pennant, 96, 146, 167, 178
Cwm Prysor, 116
Cwm Ratgoed, 153, 165
Cwm y Llan, 138
Cwm yr Wnin, 152
Cwmystradllyn, 96, 147, 167
Cwrt, 128
Cymer Abbey, 100–1, 175
Cynfal falls, 124

Daisy, ox-eye, 48, 84
Dduallt mountain, 151; station, 134
Dee river, 126, 151
Deer, fallow, 66; red, 58; roe, 58
Deganwy, 167
Devil's Kitchen, 37, 43, 75, 140, 167
Diffwys, 116, 127, 149
Dinas Dinorwig, 96
Dinas Emrys, 96, 123, 167
Dinas Mawddwy, 56, 119, 127, 153, 167–8
Dinorwig, origin of, 26
Dinorwig quarries, 108, 109, 110, 174; hydro-electric scheme, 168, 179
Dipper, 63

195

Dog's-mercury, 54, 78, 83, 84
Dolbadarn castle, 100
Dolbenmaen, 146, 168
Dolerite, 28, 42, 77, 79, 84, 143
Dôl-frwynog, 114
Dolgarrog, 145
Dolgellau, 105, 113, 114, 127, 152, 168–9
Dolgoch Falls, 131, 155
Dolmelynllyn, 127, 171
Dolmens, 91–2, 163, 169
Dolphins, 67
Dolwyddelan, 147, 169; castle, 100; slate, 109
Dormouse, 68
Dotterel, 62
Dove, turtle, 64
Drovers' roads, 105, 148, 149
Drumlins, 40
Drws-y-coed, 113, 179
Dunlin, 62, 65
Dyffryn Ardudwy, 92, 96, 149, 169
Dyfi estuary, 88–9, 118; Forest, 169; Junction, 118, 128; valley, 105, 128, 153, *168*

Eagles, 59–60
Eel, 70
Elidir Fawr, 26, 108, 141, 174
Elm, wych, 83, 84
Emperor moth, *72*, 73
Enchanter's-nightshade, 54; alpine, 57
Eryri, origin of, 15, 169
Estuaries, 56–7, 64–5
Estuary birdwatching, 64–5; fish, 70

Fairbourne, 128, 169–70
Farmlands, 22, 54–5, 64
Faults, 38–9, 161
Felwort, 88
Fern, brittle bladder, 46, 80; hard shield, 78; hart's-tongue, 83, 84; hay-scented buckler, 53; holly, 48, *49*; Killarney, 48, 53; polypody, 82; royal, 79; soft shield, 82, 84; Tunbridge filmy, 53, 79
Ferns, woodsia, 48
Fescue, dune, 88; sheep's, 48
Ffestiniog, 105, 124; hydro-electric scheme, 160; Railway, 118, 129, 132–5, *133*; Vale of, 81, 124, 135, *170*
Ffordd Cadfan, 131
Ffordd Ddu, 94, 154
Ffridd Ddu, 154
Ffwrnais (Furnace), 170–1
Ffynnon Eidda, 125
Felin Isaf, 171
Fish, coarse, 70; estuarine, 70
Flycatcher, pied, *63*, 64
Foel Fras, 143, 144, 157
Foel Goch (Glyder), 142
Foel Grach, 143
Foel y Geifr, 126, 154
Footpaths, 18, 137
Forestry Commission, 19–20, 63–4, 115, 145, 159, 169, 172
Fossils, 35
Fox, 67
Foxes' Path, 80, 161
Foxglove, 53

Friog, 118, 154, 171
Frog, 68
Frost, 16–17
Fulmar, 65
Furnace, 170–1

Gallt-yr-ogof, 32
Ganllwyd, 80, 151, 171
Garn *see* Y Garn
Garnedd Ugain, 139
Garreg, 123, 171
Geosyncline, 27, 30
Giraldus, 79
Glaciers, 39
Gladstone Rock, 138
Glan Conwy, 171
Glanllyn, 177
Glasdir mine, 113
Glasswort, 56
Gledrffordd, 144
Glen of Aran, 152
Globeflower, 48, 54
Glyder Fach, 37, 140, *141*, 171; Fawr, 9, 37, 75, 123, 140, 171; range, 26, 75, 139–42
Glyn Gywair, 126
Goats, 66, 79
Goldcrest, 64
Gold mines, 19, 116–7
Goosander, 126
Goose, whitefronted, 65, 89
Goshawk, 64
Granophyre, 79, 84
Grass, false brome, 54; marram, 87, 88; of Parnassus, 48, 54, 78; wavy hair, 76
Grasslands, mountain, 48
Grayling, 70
Great Orme, 65, 71, 175
Grebe, great-crested, 62, 65, 127; little, 62
Greenweed, hairy, 57
Grouse, red, 62, 79
Gudgeon, 70
Gull, black-headed, 62
Gulls, 65, 66
Gwydir Castle, 102, 121, 171
Gwydir Uchaf chapel, 172
Gwydyr Forest, 160, 172
Gwynfynydd mine, 116
Gwyniad, 69, *70*
Gyffyn, 165
Gylchedd, 125, 150

Happy Valley, 128, 131
Hare, 67
Harlech, 172–3; castle, 100, *102*, 172; Dome, 32, 38–9, 116
Harrier, hen, 65; marsh, 65
Hawksbeard, marsh, 83, 124
Hawk's-bit, 87
Hazel, 83, 84
Heather, 42, 50, 62, 76, 79, 81, 89, 116
Heather Terrace, 121
Helleborine, green-flowered, 88; marsh, 88, *172*
Herb-robert, 53
Heron, 76
Horsetail, variegated, 88; wood, 54
Hound's-tongue, 87